CONTENTS

ANSWER KEY

1.1. – LIMITS

Introduction:

1. $x \to \infty$ means that _____

2. $x \to -\infty$ means that _____

3. $x \to 3$ means that _____

4. $x \to 3^+$ means that _____

5. $x \to 3^-$ means that _____

6. $x \to 0^-$ means that _____

7. $x \to 0^+$ means that _____

8. $Lim\left(\dfrac{0}{\infty}\right) =$

9. $Lim\left(\dfrac{\infty}{0}\right) =$

10. $Lim\left(\dfrac{2}{3}\right) =$

11. $Lim\left(\dfrac{0^+}{\infty}\right) =$

12. $Lim\left(\dfrac{0^+}{-\infty}\right) =$

13. $Lim\left(\dfrac{-\infty}{0^-}\right) =$

14. $Lim\left(\dfrac{\infty}{\infty}\right) =$

15. $Lim\left(\dfrac{0}{0}\right) =$

16. $Lim(1^\infty) =$

17. $Lim(\infty^1) =$

18. $Lim(\infty^0) =$

19. $Lim\left(\dfrac{1}{\infty}\right) =$

20. $Lim(\infty - \infty) =$

21. $Lim(\infty + \infty) =$

22. $Lim(0 - 0) =$

23. $Lim(2 - \infty) =$

24. $Lim(0 - 5) =$

25. $Lim(\infty^{-1}) =$

5

GRAPHICAL INTERPRETATION OF LIMITS

1. Given the graph of the function:

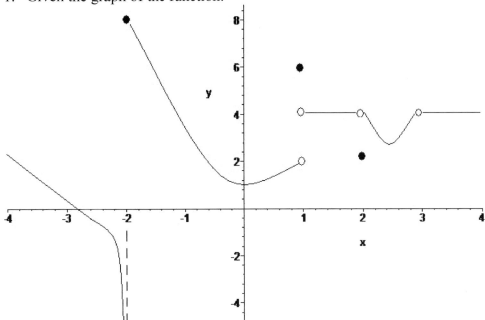

a. $\lim\limits_{x\to 0^-}(f(x))=$ $\lim\limits_{x\to 0^+}(f(x))=$ f(0) = $\lim\limits_{x\to 0}(f(x))=$

b. Since _____ the function is _____ at x = 0.

c. $\lim\limits_{x\to -3^+}(f(x))=$ $\lim\limits_{x\to -3^-}(f(x))=$ $f(3)=$ $\lim\limits_{x\to -3}(f(x))=$

d. Since_____ the function is _____ at x = −3.

e. $\lim\limits_{x\to -2^+}(f(x))=$ $\lim\limits_{x\to -2^-}(f(x))=$ $f(-2)=$ $\lim\limits_{x\to -2}(f(x))=$

f. Since _____ and _____the function

    has _____ at x= −2.

g. $\lim\limits_{x\to 1^-}(f(x))=$ $\lim\limits_{x\to 1^+}(f(x))=$ $f(1)=$ $\lim\limits_{x\to 1}(f(x))=$

h. Since _____ and _____the function

    has _____ at x = 1

i. $\lim\limits_{x\to 2^+}(f(x))=$ $\lim\limits_{x\to 2^-}(f(x))=$ $f(2)=$ $\lim\limits_{x\to 2}(f(x))=$

j. Since _____ and _____the function

    has _____ at x = 2.

k. Using the graph find all the values of a for which f(a) does not exist: _____

6

2. Given the graph of the function:

a. $\lim\limits_{x \to 0^-}(f(x)) =$

b. $\lim\limits_{x \to 0^+}(f(x)) =$

c. $\lim\limits_{x \to 0}(f(x)) =$

d. $\lim\limits_{x \to -3^+}(f(x)) =$

e. $\lim\limits_{x \to -3^-}(f(x)) =$

f. $\lim\limits_{x \to -3}(f(x)) =$

g. $f(-3) =$

h. $\lim\limits_{x \to 3^+}(f(x)) =$

i. $\lim\limits_{x \to 3^-}(f(x)) =$

j. $\lim\limits_{x \to 3}(f(x)) =$

k. $f(3) =$

l. $\lim\limits_{x \to -1^-}(f(x)) =$

m. $\lim\limits_{x \to -1^+}(f(x)) =$

n. $\lim\limits_{x \to -1}(f(x)) =$

o. $f(-1) =$

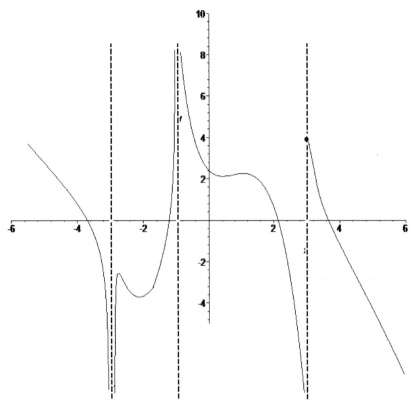

l. State the equations of all the asymptotes: _____

m. State all the points with discontinuities and the kind of discontinuity.

3. Find the following <u>limits</u>:

$\lim\limits_{x \to \infty}(f(x)) =$

$\lim\limits_{x \to \infty}(f(x)) =$

$\lim\limits_{x \to \infty}(f(x)) =$

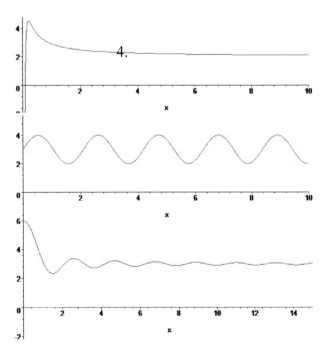

5. Find the limits:

$$\lim_{x \to -\infty} (f(x)) =$$

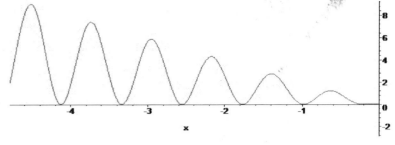

$$\lim_{x \to \infty} (f(x)) =$$

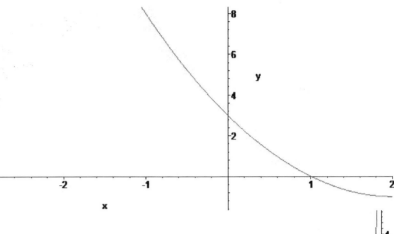

$$\lim_{x \to -\infty} (f(x)) =$$

$$\lim_{x \to -\infty} (f(x)) =$$

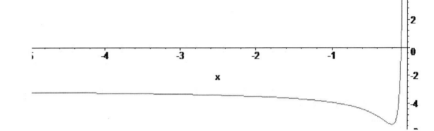

6. Horizontal asymptotes appear _____, in case we look for them

   we need to check the limit of the function when x tends to _____ or _____

7. Vertical asymptotes appear _____. We check lateral limits to

   see the behaviour of the function next to it.

THE "SQUEEZE" THEOREM

If we know that the value of a certain function f for a certain value of x satisfies
$p(a) = M \le f(a) \le q(a) = N$ it means $M \le f(a) \le N$.

For example: in case we want to find the limit $Lim_{x \to \infty} (\dfrac{e^{\sin(x)}}{x})$

$e^{-1} \le e^{\sin(x)} \le e^{1}$, divide both sides by x gives

$Lim_{x \to \infty} \left(\dfrac{e^{-1}}{x} \right) = 0 \le Lim_{x \to \infty} \left(\dfrac{e^{\sin(x)}}{x} \right) \le Lim_{x \to \infty} \left(\dfrac{e^{1}}{x} \right) = 0$ therefore $Lim_{x \to \infty} (\dfrac{e^{\sin(x)}}{x}) = 0$

8

LIMITS TYPE $x \to \pm\infty$

1. $\displaystyle\lim_{x\to\infty}\left(\frac{2x}{x}\right)=$

2. $\displaystyle\lim_{x\to\infty}\left(\frac{2x}{x^2}\right)=$

3. $\displaystyle\lim_{x\to\infty}\left(\frac{2x^2}{x}\right)=$

4. $\displaystyle\lim_{x\to\infty}\left(\frac{2x}{x+1}\right)=$

5. $\displaystyle\lim_{x\to\infty}\left(\frac{x}{2x+10}\right)=$

6. $\displaystyle\lim_{x\to\infty}\left(\frac{2x}{3x+1}\right)=$

7. $\displaystyle\lim_{x\to\infty}\left(\frac{2x^2}{6x^3-22}\right)=$

8. $\displaystyle\lim_{x\to\infty}\left(\frac{3x^2+1}{2x-2}\right)=$

9. $\displaystyle\lim_{x\to-\infty}\left(\frac{2x^2+1}{5x^2-2}\right)=$

10. $\displaystyle\lim_{x\to\infty}\left(\frac{ax^2+1}{bx-2}\right)=$

11. $\displaystyle\lim_{x\to-\infty}\left(\frac{ax^3+4x}{bx^4+5x^2-2}\right)=$

12. $=\displaystyle\lim_{x\to-\infty}\left(\frac{ax^7+4x}{bx^7+7x^2-x}\right)=$

13. $\displaystyle\lim_{x\to-\infty}\left(\frac{\sqrt{3}x^7+4x}{-2x^7+7x^2-x}\right)=$

14. $\lim\limits_{x \to -\infty} \left(\dfrac{-2x^5 + 4x^2 + 4}{x^3 + 81x^2 - 2x} \right) =$

15. $\lim\limits_{x \to -\infty} \left(\dfrac{1}{6} \dfrac{\sqrt{35}(2x^4 + 4x^2 + 4)}{2x^4 + 81x^2 - 2x} \right) =$

16. $\lim\limits_{x \to \infty} \left(\dfrac{(x+5)^4}{(2x-4)^4} \right) =$

17. $\lim\limits_{x \to -\infty} \left(\dfrac{(4x+1)^5}{(2x-7)^5} \right) =$

18. $\lim\limits_{x \to -\infty} \left(\dfrac{(5x^2 + 2)^5}{(2x-3)^6} \right) =$

19. $\lim\limits_{x \to \infty} \left(\dfrac{(5x^2 + 2)(x+3)}{(2x-3)(x^2+1)} \right) =$

20. $\lim\limits_{x \to -\infty} \left(\dfrac{(x+2)(2x+3)}{(5x-3)(2x^2+4)} \right) =$

21. $\lim\limits_{x \to \infty} \left(\dfrac{\sqrt{x^5 + 7x}}{x^2\sqrt{2x}} \right) =$

22. $\lim\limits_{x \to \infty} \left(\dfrac{\sqrt{3x^4 - x}}{x\sqrt{5x^3}} \right) =$

23. $\lim\limits_{x \to -\infty} \left(\dfrac{\sqrt{32x^4 - 3x + 5}}{3x^2} \right) =$

24. $\lim\limits_{x \to -\infty} \left(\dfrac{x + \sqrt{2x^2 - 3}}{7x + 1} \right) =$

25. $\lim\limits_{x \to -\infty} \left(\dfrac{2x^2 + \sqrt{2x^4 - 3}}{-7x^2 + 1} \right) =$

26. $\lim\limits_{x \to \infty} \left(\dfrac{ax^n + bx^{n-1} + \ldots}{kx^m + sx^{m-1} + \ldots} \right) =$

27. $\lim\limits_{x \to \infty}\left(\dfrac{x^{40}}{2^x}\right) =$

28. $\lim\limits_{x \to \infty}\left(\dfrac{2^x}{8x^{50}}\right) =$

29. $\lim\limits_{x \to -\infty}\left(\dfrac{x^{400}}{-3^x}\right) =$

30. $\lim\limits_{x \to \infty}\left(\dfrac{\sqrt{x^3 - x}}{\sqrt{x^2 - 2x}}\right) =$

31. $\lim\limits_{x \to \infty}\left(\dfrac{\sqrt{x^3 + x}}{\sqrt{2x^3 - 2x}}\right) =$

32. $\lim\limits_{x \to -\infty}(2^x - x^{12}) =$

33. $\lim\limits_{x \to \infty}(2^x - x^{12}) =$

34. $\lim\limits_{x \to \infty}(\sqrt{x^3 - x + 2} - x + 3) =$

35. $\lim\limits_{x \to \infty}(3^x - 2^x) =$

36. $\lim\limits_{x \to -\infty}(3^x - 2^x) =$

37. $\lim\limits_{x \to \infty}(\sqrt{x} - \ln(x)) =$

38. $\lim\limits_{x \to \infty}(e^x - \ln(x)) =$

39. $\lim\limits_{x \to \infty}\left(\dfrac{6^x}{5^x}\right) =$

40. $\lim\limits_{x \to \infty}\left(\dfrac{8^x}{9^x}\right) =$

41. $\lim\limits_{x \to \infty}\left(\left(\dfrac{188}{189}\right)^x\right) =$

42. $\lim\limits_{x\to\infty}\left(\left(\dfrac{a}{b}\right)^{x}\right)=$

43. $\lim\limits_{x\to\infty}\left(\dfrac{6^{x}-4^{x}}{5^{x}+5^{-x}}\right)=$

44. $\lim\limits_{x\to-\infty}\left(\dfrac{6^{x}-4^{x}}{5^{x}+5^{-x}}\right)=$

45. $\lim\limits_{x\to\infty}\left(\dfrac{x^{5}+x+2}{e^{x}}\right)=$

46. $\lim\limits_{x\to\infty}(\sqrt{x^{2}-x+2}-x^{1.1}+3)=$

47. $\lim\limits_{x\to\infty}(\sin(x))=$

48. $\lim\limits_{x\to\infty}\left(\dfrac{\sin(x)}{x}\right)=$

49. $\lim\limits_{x\to\infty}\left(\cos\left(\dfrac{1}{x}\right)\right)=$

50. $\lim\limits_{x\to\infty}\left(\dfrac{1}{\cos(x)}\right)=$

51. $\lim\limits_{x\to\infty}\left(\dfrac{1}{\ln(x)}\right)=$

52. $\lim\limits_{x\to\infty}(\ln(x)-\ln(2x))=$

53. $\lim\limits_{x\to\infty}(x-\sqrt{x^{2}-2x+5})=$

54. $\lim\limits_{x \to \infty} \left(\dfrac{\sqrt{x^4 + 2x^3 - 3} - \sqrt{x^4 - x}}{x + 5} \right) =$

55. $\lim\limits_{x \to \infty} (\sqrt{x^2 + x} - \sqrt{x^2 - x}) =$

56. $\lim\limits_{x \to \infty} (\sqrt{x^2 + x} - \sqrt{x^2 - ax}) =$

57. $\lim\limits_{x \to \infty} (\sqrt{x^3 + x} - \sqrt{x^2 - 2x}) =$

LIMITS TYPE $x \to a$

Properties of limits

Fill the missing blanks:

a. $\lim\limits_{x \to a}(c) = \underline{\quad}, c \in R$

b. $\lim\limits_{x \to a}(x) = \underline{\quad}$

c. $\lim\limits_{x \to a}(f(x) + g(x)) = \lim\limits_{x \to a}(f(x)) + \lim\limits_{x \to a}(g(x))$, the limit of the sum is the sum of the limits.

d. $\lim\limits_{x \to a}(c(f(x))) = \underline{\quad} \lim\limits_{x \to a}(f(x)), c \in R$, constants can be taken out of the limit.

e. $\lim\limits_{x \to a}(f(x) \cdot g(x)) = \lim\limits_{x \to a}(f(x)) \cdot \lim\limits_{x \to a}(g(x))$, the limit of the product is the product of the limits.

f. $\lim\limits_{x \to a}\left(\dfrac{f(x)}{g(x)}\right) = \dfrac{\lim\limits_{x \to a}(f(x))}{\lim\limits_{x \to a}(g(x))}, \lim\limits_{x \to a}(g(x)) \neq 0$, the limit of the quotient is the quotient of the limits.

g. $\lim\limits_{x \to a}((f(x))^n) = (\lim\limits_{x \to a}(f(x)))^n, n \in R$

Exercises

Compute the following limits and indicate which properties are being used:

58. $\lim\limits_{x \to 2}((x^2 + 5)(x - 3)) =$

59. $\lim\limits_{x \to 2}((x^3 - \ln(x - 1)) + (2^x + x - 3)) =$

60. $\lim\limits_{x \to 3}\left(\dfrac{(3x^2 - 5)x}{x^3 - 4}\right) =$

61. $\lim\limits_{x \to 1}\left(((2x + \cos(\pi x))^{10}\right) =$

The following limits are given:

$$\lim_{x \to 4}(f(x)) = 3, \lim_{x \to 4}(g(x)) = -2, \lim_{x \to 4}(h(x)) = \frac{2}{5}$$

Compute the following limits:

62. $\lim_{x \to 4}(3f(x) + 4g(x)) =$

63. $\lim_{x \to 4}(f(x) - 2g(x) - h(x)) =$

64. $\lim_{x \to 4}(\sqrt{(f(x))^2 + (g(x))^4}) =$

Find the following limit:

65. $\lim_{x \to 5}\left(\dfrac{x^2 - 8x + 15}{x - 5}\right) =$

As you can see if we substitute x = 5 we obtain a fraction of the form $-$, therefore we must simplify:

$$\lim_{x \to 5}\left(\frac{x^2 - 8x + 15}{x - 5}\right) = \lim_{x \to 5}\left(\frac{(\ldots\ldots\ldots)(\ldots\ldots\ldots)}{x - 5}\right) = \lim_{x \to 5}(\ldots\ldots\ldots) =$$

66. $\lim_{x \to -2}\left(\dfrac{x^2 - x - 6}{x + 2}\right) =$

67. $\lim_{x \to -1}\left(\dfrac{3x^3 + 5x^2 + 3x}{1 + x}\right) =$

68. $\lim_{x \to -2}\left(\dfrac{-4x - 8}{2 + x}\right) =$

69. $\lim_{x \to -2}\left(\dfrac{x^3 + 8}{x^2 - 4}\right) =$

70. $\lim_{x \to 2}\left(\dfrac{-2x^4 + 1}{5x^3 - 2}\right) =$

71. $\lim_{t \to 0}\left(\dfrac{\sqrt{3 - t} - \sqrt{3}}{t}\right) =$

15

72. $\lim\limits_{h \to 0}\left(\dfrac{(h+2)^3 - 8}{h} \right) =$

73. $\lim\limits_{x \to 1}\left(\dfrac{1}{x-1} - \dfrac{2}{x^2-1} \right) =$

74. $\lim\limits_{x \to 2}\left(\dfrac{\left(\dfrac{1}{x} - \dfrac{1}{2}\right)}{x-2} \right) =$

75. $\lim\limits_{x \to 3}\left(\dfrac{\sqrt{3x+7} - 4}{x-3} \right) =$

76. $\lim\limits_{x \to 4}\left(\dfrac{\sqrt{x+5} - 3}{\sqrt{x} + 3} \right) =$

77. $\lim\limits_{x \to -1}\left(\dfrac{x^2 + 2x + 1}{x^3 + 3x^2 + 3x + 1} \right) =$

78. $\lim\limits_{x \to 0}\left(\sin(x) \right) =$

79. $\lim\limits_{x \to 0}\left(\dfrac{1}{\cos(x)} \right) =$

80. $\lim\limits_{x \to 0}\left(\dfrac{2}{3 + e^{-\frac{1}{x}}} \right) =$

81. $\lim\limits_{x \to 0}\left(\dfrac{1}{\sin(x)} \right) =$

   • Check this limit on both "sides" of 0.

82. Use software or GDC to sketch a few of the functions and observe their behavior around the relevant point.

LATERAL LIMITS

83. $\lim\limits_{x\to 0}\left(\dfrac{1}{x}\right) =$ Since this limit cannot be obtained we check the _____:

$$\lim\limits_{x\to\ldots}\left(\dfrac{1}{x}\right) = \qquad\qquad \lim\limits_{x\to\ldots}\left(\dfrac{1}{x}\right) =$$

84. $\lim\limits_{x\to 0}\left(\dfrac{x}{|x|}\right) =$ Since this limit cannot be obtained we check the _____:

$$\lim\limits_{x\to\ldots}\left(\dfrac{x}{|x|}\right) = \qquad\qquad \lim\limits_{x\to\ldots}\left(\dfrac{x}{|x|}\right) =$$

Find the following limits, if possible:

85. $\lim\limits_{x\to 0}\left(\dfrac{x-2}{|x-2|}\right) =$

86. $\lim\limits_{x\to -2}\left(\dfrac{3}{x+2}\right) =$

87. $\lim\limits_{x\to -2}\left(\dfrac{3x+6}{x+2}\right) =$

88. $\lim\limits_{x\to 2^+}\left(\dfrac{4-2x}{|4-2x|}\right) =$

89. $\lim\limits_{x\to 1^-}\left(\dfrac{\sqrt{2}-\sqrt{2}x}{|\sqrt{2}-\sqrt{2}x|}\right) =$

90. $\lim\limits_{x\to 0}\left(\dfrac{1}{x}-\dfrac{1}{|x|}\right) =$

$$\lim\limits_{x\to\ldots}\left(\dfrac{1}{x}-\dfrac{1}{|x|}\right) = \qquad\qquad \lim\limits_{x\to\ldots}\left(\dfrac{1}{x}-\dfrac{1}{|x|}\right) =$$

Lateral limits should be checked in case _____

L'HOPITAL RULE $\lim\limits_{x \to a}\left(\dfrac{f(x)}{g(x)}\right) = \lim\limits_{x \to a}\left(\dfrac{f'(x)}{g'(x)}\right)$ applies **only** if $\left(\dfrac{0}{0}\right)$ or $\left(\dfrac{\pm\infty}{\pm\infty}\right)$

91. $\lim\limits_{\theta \to 0}\left(\dfrac{\sin\theta}{\theta}\right) =$

92. $\lim\limits_{\theta \to 0}\left(\dfrac{1-\sin\theta}{\tan\theta}\right) =$

93. $\lim\limits_{x \to 0}\left(\dfrac{e^x - e^{-x} - 2x}{x - \sin(x)}\right) =$

94. $\lim\limits_{\theta \to 0}\left(\dfrac{\csc\theta - \cot\theta}{\theta\csc\theta}\right) =$

95. $\lim\limits_{x \to 0}\left(\dfrac{e^x - e^{-x} - 6x}{\sin(x)}\right) =$

96. $\lim\limits_{\theta \to 0}\left(\dfrac{1 - \cos^2(\theta)}{\theta(1 + \cos(\theta))}\right) =$

97. $\lim\limits_{x \to \infty}\left(\dfrac{a}{x\sin\left(\dfrac{1}{x}\right)}\right) =$

98. $\lim\limits_{x \to \infty}\left(\dfrac{\ln(2^x + 3^x)}{x}\right) =$

99. $\lim\limits_{\theta \to 0}\left(\dfrac{\sec\theta}{\theta\csc\theta}\right) =$

100. $\lim\limits_{t \to 0}\left(\dfrac{\sin 5t}{t}\right) =$

101. $\lim\limits_{\theta \to 0}\left(\dfrac{\sin(\cos\theta)}{\sec\theta}\right) =$

102. $\lim\limits_{\theta \to 0}\left(\dfrac{\sin^2\theta}{\theta}\right) =$

103. $\lim\limits_{x \to 0}\left(\dfrac{\cot 2x}{\csc x}\right) =$

104. $\lim\limits_{\theta \to 0}\left(\dfrac{\sin\theta}{\theta + \tan\theta}\right) =$

105. $\lim\limits_{\theta \to 0}\left(\dfrac{\tan 2\theta}{\theta}\right) =$

106. $\lim\limits_{x \to 0}\left(\dfrac{x}{1 - \sqrt{x+1}}\right) =$

107. $\lim\limits_{x \to 0}\left(\dfrac{\sqrt{1-x} - \sqrt{1+x}}{x}\right) =$

108. $\lim\limits_{x \to 1}\left(\dfrac{x^4 - 1}{x^2 - 1}\right) =$

109. $\lim\limits_{x \to 1}\left(\dfrac{x^5 - 1}{x^2 - 1}\right) =$

110. $\lim\limits_{x \to 1}\left(\dfrac{2x^2 - 4x + 2}{6x^2 - 6}\right) =$

111. $\lim\limits_{x \to \infty}\left(\dfrac{x^3 - 1}{x^2 - 1}\right) =$

112. $\lim\limits_{x \to 0}\left(\dfrac{\sin(\sin(x))}{\sin(x^2)}\right) =$

113. $\lim\limits_{x \to 1}\left(\dfrac{\ln(x)}{x - 1}\right) =$

114. $\lim\limits_{x \to 7}\left(\dfrac{x^2 - 8x + 7}{x - 7}\right) =$

115. $\lim\limits_{x \to 1}\left(\dfrac{\cos^2\left(\dfrac{\pi x}{2}\right)}{(x-1)^2}\right) =$

116. $\lim\limits_{x \to 0} \left(\dfrac{\sin(x) - \ln(x+1)}{x^2 e^x} \right) =$

117. $\lim\limits_{x \to 0} \left(\dfrac{e^x - \ln(x+e)}{\sin(2x)} \right) =$

118. $\lim\limits_{x \to 0} \left(\dfrac{e^{4x} - 2e^{2x} + 1)}{\left(\sin(3x)\right)^2} \right) =$

1.2. – SEQUENCES AND SERIES

1. The following numbers 3, 7, 11, 15, …form a _____

2. A **sequence** whose terms tend to _____ is called convergent. Otherwise the sequence is called _____

3. The corresponding **series** is 3 + 7 + _____

4. Given the following **sequences**, determine if the sequence is convergent and write the corresponding sum.

    a. 1, 2, 3, 4… Convergent / Divergent, Corresponding sum:

    b. 5, 10, 15, 20, 25, 30 Convergent / Divergent, Corresponding sum:

    c. 5, 10, 20, 40 … Convergent / Divergent, Corresponding sum:

    d. 200, –100, 50, –25, … Convergent / Divergent, Corresponding sum:

    e. $\frac{1}{2}, \frac{2}{4}, \frac{3}{8}, \frac{4}{16}$… Convergent / Divergent, Corresponding sum:

    f. 12, 10, 8, 6… –100. Convergent / Divergent, Corresponding sum:

    g. 10, 1, 0.1, 0.01, 0.001, 0.0001 Convergent / Divergent, Corresponding sum:

    h. $\frac{1}{1}, \frac{1}{2}, \frac{1}{3}, \frac{1}{4}, ..., \frac{1}{122}$ Convergent / Divergent, Corresponding sum:

    i. $\frac{7}{5}, -\frac{7}{10}, \frac{7}{20}, -\frac{7}{40}, ..., \frac{7}{1280}$ Convergent / Divergent, Corresponding sum:

    j. 6, 10, 14, …,118 Convergent / Divergent, Corresponding sum:

5. **Series** are often written using _____.

   For example the series $3 + 7 + 11 + 15 + \dots$ can be written: $\displaystyle\sum_{k=1}^{\infty} 4k - 1$

6. Write the following **series** using sigma notation, if the series is arithmetic or geometric, find the sum:

   k. $1 + 2 + 3 + 4\dots. =$ _____

   l. $1 + 2 + 3 + 4 =$ _____

   m. $5 + 10 + 15 + 20 + 25 + 30 =$ _____

   n. $5 + 10 + 20 + 40 + \dots =$ _____

   o. $200 - 100 + 50 - 25 + \dots =$ _____

   p. $\dfrac{1}{2} + \dfrac{2}{4} + \dfrac{3}{8} + \dfrac{4}{16} + \dots =$ _____

   q. $12 + 10 + 8 + \dots -100 =$ _____

   r. $10 + 1 + 0.1 + 0.01 + 0.001 + 0.0001 =$ _____

   s. $\dfrac{1}{1} + \dfrac{1}{2} + \dfrac{1}{3} + \dfrac{1}{4} + \dots + \dfrac{1}{122} =$ _____

   t. $\dfrac{7}{5} - \dfrac{7}{10} + \dfrac{7}{20} - \dfrac{7}{40} + \dots \dfrac{7}{1280} =$ _____

   u. $6 + 10 + 14 + \dots + 118 =$ _____

   v. $\dfrac{1}{e} - \dfrac{1}{e^2} + \dfrac{1}{e^3} - \dfrac{1}{e^4} + \dots =$ _____

7. Write each series using sigma notation:

    a. $1 + 8 + 27 + 81 + \ldots = \displaystyle\sum_{i=\_}^{i=\_}$ _____

    b. $15 + 19 + 23 + 27 + 31 + 35 + 39 + 43 = \displaystyle\sum_{i=\_}^{i=\_}$ _____

    c. $1 + \dfrac{1}{9} + \dfrac{1}{81} + \ldots = \displaystyle\sum_{i=\_}^{i=\_}$ _____

8. Use sigma notation to represent $13 + 16 + 19 + 22 + \ldots$ for 28 terms. Sum the terms.

$$\sum_{i=\_}^{i=\_}$$ _____

9. Use sigma notation to represent $-30 + 60 - 120 + 240 - 480 + \ldots$ for 35 terms. Sum the terms.

$$\sum_{i=\_}^{i=\_}$$ _____

10. Use sigma notation to represent: $18.13 + 18.11 + 18.09 + 18.07 + \ldots$ for 100 terms. Sum the terms

$$\sum_{i=\_}^{i=\_}$$ _____

11. The following **sequence** $1, \frac{1}{2}, \frac{1}{3}, \frac{1}{4}, \ldots$ is _____ (its terms tend to 0). Its

corresponding series $\sum_{n=1}^{\infty} \frac{1}{n} = 1 + \frac{1}{2} + \frac{1}{3} + \frac{1}{4} + \ldots$ is called the _____

series. It is **divergent**, which means the sum **does not add up to** _____.

12. So as can be seen in the previous example even if the general term of a sequence

tends to ____ it does not mean the corresponding series will add up to a _____

(that is, will be convergent).

13. The following **sequence** $1, \frac{1}{4}, \frac{1}{9}, \frac{1}{16}, \ldots$ is _____ (its terms tend to 0). The

corresponding series $\sum_{n=1}^{\infty} \frac{1}{n^2} = 1 + \frac{1}{4} + \frac{1}{9} + \frac{1}{16} + \ldots$, (calculated by Leonard Euler)

is **convergent**, which means the sum **adds up to** _____. In fact this

is a famous sum the as Euler proved adds up to $\frac{\pi^2}{6}$

14. A series is convergent if _____

15. A series is divergent if _____

16. If the general term of a **sequence** tends to 0 the **corresponding series** may be

_____ or _____.

17. If the general term of a **sequence** does not tend to 0 the **corresponding series**

will be _____

18. Determine if the general term tends to 0 and in consequence write down which
    of the following series diverge. In those the general term does not tend to 0 try to
    deduce if the series converge or diverge.

a. $\sum_{n=1}^{\infty} \frac{2n}{3n+1}$ $Lim_{n \to \infty} \left(\frac{2n}{3n+1} \right) =$

b. $\sum_{n=1}^{\infty} \frac{n}{3n^2 + n + 2} =$

c. $\displaystyle\sum_{n=2}^{\infty} 1 + \frac{1}{\ln(n)} =$

d. $\displaystyle\sum_{n=1}^{\infty} 5\frac{3^{n+3}}{4^{n-1}} =$

e. $\displaystyle\sum_{n=1}^{\infty} n+1 =$

f. $\displaystyle\sum_{n=1}^{\infty} \frac{5\sqrt{n}+1}{\sqrt{n}} =$

g. $\displaystyle\sum_{n=1}^{\infty} \frac{5n}{n^{\frac{5}{3}}\sqrt{n}} =$

h. $\displaystyle\sum_{n=1}^{\infty} \frac{6^{n+3}+2^{n}+1}{5^{n-1}} =$

i. $\displaystyle\sum_{n=1}^{\infty} \frac{\sin(\pi n)}{n^2} =$

j. $\displaystyle\sum_{n=1}^{\infty} \frac{\cos(\pi n)}{n^2} =$

k. $\displaystyle\sum_{n=1}^{\infty} \frac{\cos(\pi n)}{2^n} =$

l. $\displaystyle\sum_{n=1}^{\infty} \frac{8}{9^n} =$

m. $\displaystyle\sum_{n=1}^{\infty} \frac{\cos\left(\frac{1}{n}\right)}{n} =$

1.3. – THE P-SERIES

1. The **series** $\sum_{n=1}^{\infty} \dfrac{1}{n^p} = 1 + \dfrac{1}{2^p} + \dfrac{1}{3^p} + \dfrac{1}{4^p} + \ldots$ is called the _____

2. This series was studied a lot and the following conclusions deduced:

   If _____ it is **divergent**, which means the sum **does not add up to** _____

   If _____ it is **convergent**, which means the sum **adds up to** _____

3. If p = 1 it is called the _____ series.

Determine if the following series converge or diverge:

4. $\sum_{n=1}^{n=\infty} n$

5. $\sum_{n=1}^{n=\infty} \dfrac{1}{\sqrt{n}}$

6. $\sum_{n=1}^{n=\infty} \dfrac{1}{\sqrt[3]{n}}$

7. $\sum_{n=1}^{n=\infty} \dfrac{1}{n^3}$

8. $\sum_{n=1}^{n=\infty} \dfrac{1}{n^{0.999}}$

9. $\sum_{n=1}^{n=\infty} \dfrac{1}{n\sqrt{n}}$

10. $\sum_{n=1}^{n=\infty} \dfrac{1}{n^{\frac{20}{31}}}$

11. $\sum_{n=1}^{n=\infty} \dfrac{1}{\sqrt[17]{n^2}}$

12. $\sum_{n=1}^{n=\infty} \dfrac{1}{\sqrt[7]{n^2}\, n^{0.80}}$

13. $\sum_{n=1}^{n=\infty} \dfrac{1}{n}$

14. $\sum_{n=1}^{n=\infty} \left(\dfrac{1}{2}\right)^n$

15. $\sum_{n=1}^{n=\infty} e^n$

16. $\sum_{n=1}^{n=\infty} \sin(n)$

17. $\displaystyle\sum_{n=1}^{n=\infty} \frac{1}{n^2}$

18. $\displaystyle\sum_{n=1}^{n=\infty} 5\left(\frac{2}{3}\right)^n$

19. $\displaystyle\sum_{n=1}^{n=\infty} 2n+1$

20. $\displaystyle\sum_{n=1}^{n=\infty} \sqrt{n}$

21. $\displaystyle\sum_{n=1}^{n=\infty} \ln(n)$

22. $\displaystyle\sum_{n=1}^{n=\infty} \sin(\frac{1}{n})$

23. $\displaystyle\sum_{n=1}^{n=\infty} 2\left(\frac{7}{6}\right)^n$

24. $\displaystyle\sum_{n=1}^{n=\infty} \ln(\frac{1}{n})$

25. $\displaystyle\sum_{n=1}^{n=\infty} 1200\left(-\frac{1}{6}\right)^n$

26. $\displaystyle\sum_{n=1}^{n=\infty} e^{\frac{1}{n}}$

27. $\displaystyle\sum_{n=1}^{n=\infty} 2^n$

28. $\displaystyle\sum_{n=1}^{n=\infty} \left(-\frac{11}{8}\right)^n$

29. $\displaystyle\sum_{n=1}^{\infty} \frac{2n}{3n^2} =$

30. $\displaystyle\sum_{n=1}^{\infty} \frac{n^2}{5n^2+2} =$

31. $\displaystyle\sum_{n=2}^{\infty} \frac{\sqrt{n}}{\sqrt[3]{n}} =$

32. $\displaystyle\sum_{n=1}^{n=\infty} 2^{-n}$

33. $\displaystyle\sum_{n=1}^{\infty} \frac{n^2+n}{3n^3} =$

34. $\displaystyle\sum_{n=1}^{\infty} \frac{n\sqrt{n^3}}{2\sqrt{n}\cdot n^2} =$

35. $\displaystyle\sum_{n=1}^{\infty} \frac{3n^2+2n+1}{5n^2+3n+4} =$

36. $\displaystyle\sum_{n=1}^{\infty} \frac{\sin(n\pi)+n^2}{-n^4} =$

37. $\displaystyle\sum_{n=1}^{\infty} \frac{\cos(n\pi)-n^2}{n^3} =$

38. $\displaystyle\sum_{n=1}^{\infty} \frac{8\sqrt[5]{n}\cdot n^2}{5n\sqrt[3]{n}} =$

1.4. – CONVERGENCE TESTS

1. In order to check if a certain series converges or diverges we will use one of the following tests:

Name of Test	How to use it	Consequence
N^{th} Term Test	Check the limit $Lim_{n \to \infty} (a_n)$	If $Lim_{n \to \infty} (a_n) \neq 0 \Rightarrow$ Divergent If $Lim_{n \to \infty} (a_n) = 0 \Rightarrow$ Inconclusive, use the next test.
Geometric Series Test	Is it a Geometric Series? If it is check the ratio, if not, use the next test	If $|r| \geq 1$ Divergent If $|r| \leq 1$ Convergent
P – Series Test	Is it a p-series Series? If it is check the value of p, if not, use the next test	If $p \leq 1$ Divergent If $p > 1$ Convergent
Comparison Test	Can I compare the series with a series that I am familiar with? Typically with a p-series or a geometric	If $\sum\limits_{n=1}^{n=\infty} a_n \geq$ Divergent, it will diverge If $\sum\limits_{n=1}^{n=\infty} a_n \leq$ Convergent, it will converge, otherwise inconclusive
Ratio Test	Find the limit $Lim_{n \to \infty} \left| \dfrac{a_{n+1}}{a_n} \right| = L$	If L < 1 Convergent If L > 1 Convergent If L = 1 Inconclusive (another test)
Alternating	Is the series alternating? If yes check, if not use a different test	$Lim_{n \to \infty} (a_n) = 0 \Rightarrow$ Convergent
Limit Comparison Test	Find the limit $Lim_{n \to \infty} \left| \dfrac{a_n}{b_n} \right| = C \Rightarrow$ Divide a_n is the general term, b_n is a general term of a series <u>whose behaviour is known</u> (we know if it converges or diverges), typically a p-series or a geometric series	If $Lim_{n \to \infty} \left| \dfrac{a_n}{b_n} \right| = C > 0 \Rightarrow$ Series have the same behaviour If $Lim_{n \to \infty} \left| \dfrac{a_n}{b_n} \right| = 0$ or $\pm \infty \Rightarrow$ Inconclusive
Integral Test	Can the general term be integrated if it can, integrate it and check (the function must be continuous and positive), if not use the next test	If $\int\limits_{b}^{\infty} a_n$ converges, series converges If $\int\limits_{b}^{\infty} a_n$ diverges, series diverges

Determine if the following series converge or diverge:

2. Use the Comparison Test to determine, if possible, convergence/divergence of the series, comment if other tests are more suitable.

a. $\displaystyle\sum_{n=1}^{n=\infty} \frac{2}{n+1}$

b. $\displaystyle\sum_{n=1}^{n=\infty} \frac{1}{n-1}$

c. $\displaystyle\sum_{n=1}^{n=\infty} \frac{1}{n \cdot 2^n}$

d. $\displaystyle\sum_{n=1}^{n=\infty} \frac{2^n}{\ln(2)}$

e. $\displaystyle\sum_{n=1}^{n=\infty} \frac{1}{\ln(n) \cdot 3^n}$

f. $\displaystyle\sum_{n=1}^{n=\infty} \frac{n+2}{n+1}$

g. $\displaystyle\sum_{n=1}^{n=\infty} \frac{5}{3^{n-1}+n}$

h. $\displaystyle\sum_{n=1}^{n=\infty} \frac{1}{\ln(n)(0.5)^{n-1}e^n}$

3. Use the Ratio Test to determine, if possible, convergence/divergence of the series, comment if other tests are more suitable.

a. $\displaystyle\sum_{n=1}^{n=\infty} \frac{1}{n!}$

b. $\displaystyle\sum_{n=1}^{n=\infty} \frac{2^n}{n}$

c. $\displaystyle\sum_{n=1}^{n=\infty} \frac{1}{\ln(n)}$

d. $\displaystyle\sum_{n=1}^{n=\infty} \frac{n}{3^{n+1}}(-1)^n$

e. $\displaystyle\sum_{n=1}^{n=\infty} \frac{1}{\sqrt{n}}$

f. $\displaystyle\sum_{n=1}^{n=\infty} n!$

g. $\displaystyle\sum_{n=1}^{n=\infty} \frac{1}{n \cdot 3^{n+1}}$

h. $\displaystyle\sum_{n=1}^{n=\infty} \frac{n!}{5^n}$

i. $\displaystyle\sum_{n=1}^{n=\infty} \frac{1}{2^{n+1}\sqrt{n}}$

j. $\displaystyle\sum_{n=1}^{n=\infty} \frac{(-1)^n}{3^n \sqrt[3]{n}}$

k. $\displaystyle\sum_{n=1}^{n=\infty} \frac{n!}{n^n}$

l. $\displaystyle\sum_{n=1}^{n=\infty} \frac{n}{\ln(n)2^{n}}$

m. $\displaystyle\sum_{n=1}^{n=\infty} \frac{\ln(n)}{2^{\sqrt{n}}}$

4. Use the Limit Comparison Test to determine, if possible, convergence/divergence of the series, comment if other tests are more suitable.

a. $\displaystyle\sum_{n=1}^{n=\infty} \frac{1}{n+1}$

b. $\displaystyle\sum_{n=1}^{n=\infty} \frac{\sqrt{n}}{3n^{2}+3}$

c. $\displaystyle\sum_{n=1}^{n=\infty} \frac{n^{2}+4n}{2n^{4}+3n+1}$ ç

d. $\displaystyle\sum_{n=1}^{n=\infty} \frac{1}{3n+2^{n}}$

e. $\displaystyle\sum_{n=1}^{n=\infty} \frac{1}{3n+2^{n}}$

f. $\displaystyle\sum_{n=1}^{n=\infty} \frac{\cos(n\pi)}{3n+\sin(n)}$

g. $\displaystyle\sum_{n=1}^{n=\infty} \frac{\sqrt{n}}{5+n+\ln(n)}$

h. $\displaystyle\sum_{n=1}^{n=\infty} \frac{3^{n}}{2^{n}+n+\ln(n)}$

5. Use the Integral Test to determine, if possible, convergence/divergence of the series, comment if other tests are more suitable. (This part can be done only after integration was taught)

a. $\displaystyle\sum_{n=1}^{n=\infty} \frac{1}{n^3}$

b. $\displaystyle\sum_{n=1}^{n=\infty} \frac{1}{n^{0.9}}$

c. $\displaystyle\sum_{n=1}^{n=\infty} \frac{1}{n\ln(n)}$

d. $\displaystyle\sum_{n=1}^{n=\infty} 2^{-n}$

e. $\displaystyle\sum_{n=1}^{n=\infty} \frac{\sin(n^{-1})}{n^2}$

f. $\displaystyle\sum_{n=1}^{n=\infty} \frac{1}{\sqrt[7]{n^2}\, n^{0.80}}$

g. $\displaystyle\sum_{n=1}^{n=\infty} \frac{1}{2n-5}$

h. $\displaystyle\sum_{n=1}^{n=\infty} \left(\frac{1}{2}\right)^n$

i. $\displaystyle\sum_{n=1}^{n=\infty} e^{-n}\ln(e^{-n}+1)$

j. $\displaystyle\sum_{n=1}^{n=\infty} 2^{-n}\sin(2^{-n})$

k. $\displaystyle\sum_{n=1}^{n=\infty} \frac{1}{n^2+1}$

l. $\displaystyle\sum_{n=1}^{n=\infty} \frac{n}{\sqrt{n^2-5}}$

m. $\displaystyle\sum_{n=1}^{n=\infty} \frac{Ln(2+\frac{1}{n})}{n^2}$

6. Use a Test to determine, if possible, convergence/divergence of the series:

a. $\displaystyle\sum_{n=1}^{n=\infty} \frac{\sqrt{n}}{n^3}$

b. $\displaystyle\sum_{n=1}^{n=\infty} \frac{1}{\ln(n)}$

c. $\displaystyle\sum_{n=1}^{n=\infty} \ln(n^{-1}+1)$

d. $\displaystyle\sum_{n=1}^{n=\infty} \tan(\frac{1}{n})$

e. $\displaystyle\sum_{n=1}^{n=\infty} 12\cdot\left(\frac{81}{80}\right)^n$

f. $\displaystyle\sum_{n=1}^{n=\infty} (-1)^n \ln(\frac{1}{n})$

g. $\displaystyle\sum_{n=1}^{n=\infty} (-1)^n \ln(\frac{1}{n}+1)$

h. $\displaystyle\sum_{n=1}^{n=\infty} (-1)^n \sqrt{\sin(\frac{1}{n})}$

i. $\displaystyle\sum_{n=1}^{n=\infty} \frac{\cos(n\pi)+e^{i\pi n}}{n}$

j. $\displaystyle\sum_{n=1}^{n=\infty} \frac{1}{n+\ln(n)}$

k. $\displaystyle\sum_{n=1}^{n=\infty} \frac{1}{n(\ln(n))^2}$

l. $\displaystyle\sum_{n=1}^{n=\infty} \frac{1}{n+\sin(n)}$

m. $\displaystyle\sum_{n=1}^{n=\infty} \frac{n}{n-2^n}$

n. $\displaystyle\sum_{n=1}^{n=\infty} \frac{n-\dfrac{1}{n}}{n+\dfrac{1}{n}}$

1. The **series** $\sum_{n=1}^{\infty} a_n$ is called absolutely convergent if $\sum_{n=1}^{\infty} |a_n|$ is _____

2. The **series** $\sum_{n=1}^{\infty} a_n$ is called conditionally convergent if $\sum_{n=1}^{\infty} |a_n|$ is divergent but

$\sum_{n=1}^{\infty} a_n$ is _____.

3. An alternating series is a series of the form:

$$\sum_{n=1}^{\infty}(-1)^n a_n \quad \text{or} \quad \sum_{n=1}^{\infty}(-1)^{n-1} a_n \quad \text{or} \quad \sum_{n=1}^{\infty}\cos(n\pi)a_n$$

4. An alternating series will converge if $Lim_{n\to\infty}(a_n)=0$

5. For example the series: $\sum_{n=1}^{\infty}\dfrac{1}{n}$ is _____. However the series

$\sum_{n=1}^{\infty}(-1)^n\dfrac{1}{n}$ is alternating, its general term tends to _____ and therefore it is

_____. We can say that $\sum_{n=1}^{\infty}(-1)^n\dfrac{1}{n}$ is _____ convergent.

Determine if the following series are conditionally convergent, absolutely convergent or divergent:

6. $\sum_{n=1}^{n=\infty}\dfrac{1}{n^3}$

7. $\sum_{n=1}^{n=\infty}(-1)^n\dfrac{1}{\sqrt[5]{n}}$

8. $\sum_{n=1}^{n=\infty}\cos(n\pi)$

9. $\sum_{n=1}^{n=\infty}(-1)^{1000+n}\dfrac{1}{n^{0.999}}$

10. $\sum_{n=1}^{n=\infty}1+\dfrac{1}{n\sqrt{n}}$

11. $\displaystyle\sum_{n=1}^{n=\infty}(-1)^n\,\dfrac{1}{n^{\frac{32}{31}}}$

12. $\displaystyle\sum_{n=1}^{n=\infty}\dfrac{\sin(n\pi)}{\sqrt[7]{n^2}}$

13. $\displaystyle\sum_{n=1}^{n=\infty}(-5)^n$

14. $\displaystyle\sum_{n=1}^{n=\infty}\dfrac{(-2)^n}{n}$

15. $\displaystyle\sum_{n=1}^{n=\infty}\left(\dfrac{1}{2}\right)^n$

16. $\displaystyle\sum_{n=1}^{n=\infty}(-0.9)^n$

17. $\displaystyle\sum_{n=1}^{n=\infty}\dfrac{(-1)^n\sin(n)}{n}$

18. $\displaystyle\sum_{n=1}^{n=\infty}1+\dfrac{3}{n^2}$

19. $\displaystyle\sum_{n=1}^{n=\infty}5\cdot\left(\dfrac{7}{9}\right)^n$

20. $\displaystyle\sum_{n=1}^{n=\infty}\cos(n\pi+\dfrac{\pi}{2})\sqrt{2n+1}$

21. $\displaystyle\sum_{n=1}^{n=\infty}(-1)^n\sqrt{n}$

22. $\displaystyle\sum_{n=1}^{n=\infty}5\cdot\big(\ln(n)-\ln(2n)\big)^n$

23. $\displaystyle\sum_{n=1}^{n=\infty}\sin(\dfrac{1}{n}-n\pi)$

24. $\displaystyle\sum_{n=1}^{n=\infty}\dfrac{\sin(e^{\frac{1}{n}})}{n^2}$

25. $\displaystyle\sum_{n=1}^{n=\infty} \frac{(-1)^n}{\ln(\ln(n))}$

26. $\displaystyle\sum_{n=1}^{n=\infty} \frac{1200(-2)^n}{n \cdot 2^n}$

27. $\displaystyle\sum_{n=1}^{n=\infty} e^{-\frac{1}{n}}$

28. $\displaystyle\sum_{n=1}^{n=\infty} 2^{n\ln(n)-n\ln(2n)}$

29. $\displaystyle\sum_{n=1}^{n=\infty} \left(-\frac{11}{10}\right)^{n+12}$

30. $\displaystyle\sum_{n=1}^{\infty} \frac{2n+2}{3n+1} =$

31. $\displaystyle\sum_{n=1}^{\infty} \frac{\ln(e^n)}{n} =$

32. $\displaystyle\sum_{n=2}^{\infty} \frac{\cos(e^{\frac{1}{n}})}{\sqrt[3]{n}} =$

33. $\displaystyle\sum_{n=1}^{n=\infty} (-1)^n \, 2^{-n}$

34. $\displaystyle\sum_{n=1}^{\infty} (-1)^n \frac{n^2+n}{3n^3} =$

35. $\displaystyle\sum_{n=1}^{\infty} \frac{n\sqrt{n^3}}{2\sqrt{n} \cdot n^2}(-1)^n$

36. $\displaystyle\sum_{n=1}^{\infty} Ln\left(\frac{3n^2+2n+1}{5n^2+3n+4}\right) =$

37. $\displaystyle\sum_{n=1}^{\infty} \frac{\cos(n\pi)+n^2}{-n^4} =$

38. $\displaystyle\sum_{n=1}^{\infty} \frac{\cos(n\pi)}{\sqrt{n^3}} =$

1.6. – POWER SERIES

1. In occasions it is more comfortable to write a certain function, for example $\sin(x)$, $\cos(x)$ or $e^{(x^2)}$ as an infinite sum of monomials or a power series. In consequence the aspect of a power series is:

$$\sum_{n=1}^{\infty} a_n x^n \text{ (center is at 0)} \qquad \text{or} \qquad \sum_{n=1}^{\infty} a_n (x-c)^n \text{ (center is at c)}$$

2. For example the function $f(x) = e^x$ can be written as a power series as follows. If we choose to approximate around 0:

Degree: 0

$$f(x) = e^x \approx 1$$

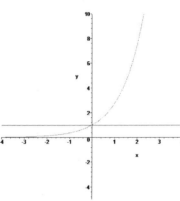

Degree: 1

$$f(x) = e^x \approx 1 + x$$

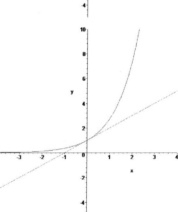

Degree: 2

$$f(x) = e^x \approx 1 + x + \frac{1}{2}x^2$$

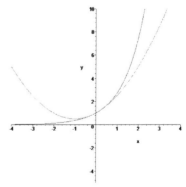

Degree: 3

$$f(x) = e^x \approx 1 + x + \frac{1}{2}x^2 + \frac{1}{6}x^3$$

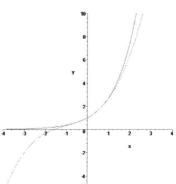

3. The value of the approximation is perfect at x = _____ and differs from it for values that are away from it.

4. In case we approximate the same function around 1:

Degree: 0

$$f(x) = e^x \approx e$$

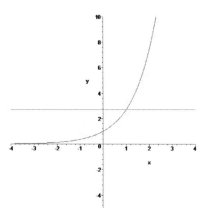

Degree: 1

$$f(x) = e^x \approx e + e(x-1)$$

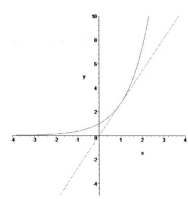

Degree: 2

$$f(x) = e^x \approx e + e(x-1) + \frac{e}{2}(x-1)^2$$

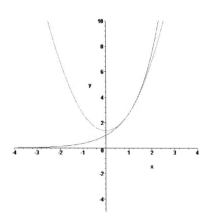

Degree: 3

$$f(x) = e^x \approx e + e(x-1) + \frac{e}{2}(x-1)^2 + \frac{e}{6}(x-1)^3$$

As can be seen, here the approximation is perfect at x = e. The higher the degree of approximation is the better the approximation is.

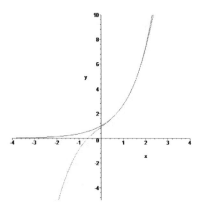

Given the following series, determine their centre and write down the coefficient:

5. $\displaystyle\sum_{n=1}^{n=\infty} x^n$ Centre: _____ $a_n =$ _____

6. $\displaystyle\sum_{n=1}^{n=\infty} \frac{1}{n}(x+2)^n$ Centre: _____ $a_n =$ _____

7. $\displaystyle\sum_{n=1}^{n=\infty} \frac{x^n}{\sqrt{n}}$ Centre: _____ $a_n =$ _____

8. $\displaystyle\sum_{n=1}^{n=\infty} (n+1)(x-2)^n \frac{1}{\sqrt[3]{n}}$ Centre: _____ $a_n =$ _____

9. $\displaystyle\sum_{n=1}^{n=\infty} \frac{\sin(n)x^n}{n^3}$ Centre: _____ $a_n =$ _____

10. $\displaystyle\sum_{k=1}^{k=\infty} \frac{\ln(k)(2x+6)^k}{k^{0.999}}$ Centre: _____ $a_n =$ _____

11. $\displaystyle\sum_{n=1}^{n=\infty} \frac{3^n \left(3x\right)^n}{\sqrt{n}}$ Centre: _____ $a_n =$ _____

12. $\displaystyle\sum_{n=1}^{n=\infty} \frac{(1-x)^n}{n\ln(n)}$ Centre: _____ $a_n =$ _____

Given the graph of the approximation, write down the centre of the power series

13. Centre: _____   14. Centre: _____

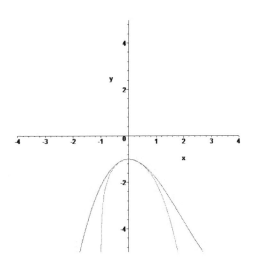

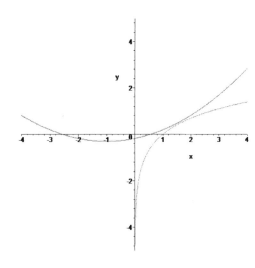

15. A power series may not produce a finite value for any value of x, the set of values for which it produces a finite value is called the interval of convergence.

Example 1: The series $\sum\limits_{n=1}^{n=\infty} \dfrac{(-1)^n}{n!} x^n$ whose centre is x = 0 will produce a finite

value for any x. Its interval of convergence there for is $(-\infty,\infty)$ and its radius of convergence $R = \infty$

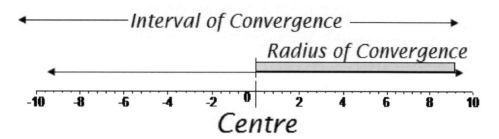

Example 2: The series $\sum\limits_{n=1}^{n=\infty} \dfrac{(-1)^n}{2^n} (x-1)^n$ whose centre is x = 1 will produce a

finite value for x between −1 and 3. Its interval of convergence there for is $(-1,3)$ and its radius of convergence is $R = 2$

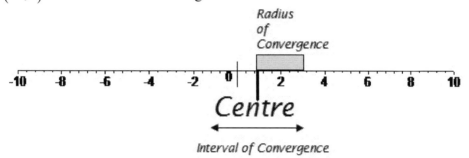

How are the Interval of Convergence and Radius of Convergence determined? We use the ratio Test

Example: Taking the same series: $\sum\limits_{n=1}^{n=\infty} \dfrac{(-1)^n}{2^n} (x-1)^n$ applying the ratio test and

imposing Ratio < 1 (in which case the power series will converge):

$$Lim_{n\to\infty} \left| \dfrac{\dfrac{(-1)^{n+1}}{2^{n+1}}(x-1)^{n+1}}{\dfrac{(-1)^n}{2^n}(x-1)^n} \right| = Lim_{n\to\infty} \left| \dfrac{(-1)^1}{2^1}(x-1)^1 \right| = \left| \dfrac{x-1}{2} \right| < 1, \text{ solving: } \begin{array}{c} |x-1| < 2 \\ -1 < x < 3 \end{array}$$

Important Note: When x = −1 or 3 the series may converge or diverge, these cases must be checked separately:

Plugging x = -1: $\sum\limits_{n=1}^{n=\infty} \dfrac{(-1)^n}{2^n}(-2)^n = \sum\limits_{n=1}^{n=\infty} 1 = n \to \infty$ so divergent

Plugging x = 3: $\sum\limits_{n=1}^{n=\infty} \dfrac{(-1)^n}{2^n}(2)^n = \sum\limits_{n=1}^{n=\infty} (-1)^n = 1-1+1-1... $ so divergent

Find the Centre, Interval of Convergence and Radius of Convergence of the following power series:

16. $\displaystyle\sum_{n=1}^{n=\infty} e^{-n}x^n$

17. $\displaystyle\sum_{n=1}^{n=\infty} \frac{n(x+4)^n}{2^n}$

18. $\displaystyle\sum_{n=1}^{n=\infty} \frac{2^n}{n^2}(x-2)^n$

19. $\displaystyle\sum_{n=1}^{n=\infty} \frac{3}{4^n n^2}(x+1)^n$

20. $\displaystyle\sum_{n=1}^{n=\infty} \frac{n^n}{n!}x^n$

21. $\displaystyle\sum_{n=1}^{n=\infty} \frac{n}{3^{n+1}\ln(n)}(x+5)^n$

22. $\displaystyle\sum_{n=1}^{n=\infty} \frac{n}{\left(Ln(n)\right)^n}(x-2)^n$

23. $\displaystyle\sum_{n=1}^{n=\infty} \frac{2n^2}{5^{n+1}}(2x-2)^n$

24. $\displaystyle\sum_{n=1}^{n=\infty} \frac{n+1}{8^n}(4x-2)^n$

25. $\displaystyle\sum_{n=1}^{n=\infty} \frac{(n+1)}{\ln(n)+5^n}x^n$

1.7. –TAYLOR AND MCLAURIN SERIES

1. In the 18th century The Taylor series (which are power series) used to approximate values of functions were developed. The English Brook Taylor came up with the following formula:

$$f(a) = f(a) + f'(a)(x-a) + \frac{1}{2!}f''(a)(x-a)^2 + \frac{1}{3!}f'''(a)(x-a)^3 + ...$$

Or $\quad f(a) = \sum_{n=0}^{\infty} \frac{f^n(a)(x-a)^n}{n!}$

2. When the value around which (a) the series is developed is 0, it is called a

    _____ series.

3. Find the Taylor Series for sin(x) around the point x = 0. Find 3 – 4 terms, identify the pattern and write it in sigma notation.

4. Find the Mclaurin Series for cos(x). Find 3 – 4 terms, identify the pattern and write it in sigma notation.

5. What would be the Taylor Series of $f(x) = 3x^4 + x^3 + 5$ around x = 0?

6. Find the Taylor Series for $f(x) = e^x$ up to 3rd degree around the point x = 1

7. Find the Taylor Series for $f(x) = \ln(x)$ up to 3rd degree around the point x = 1

8. Find the Taylor Series for $f(x) = \sqrt{x}$ up to 3rd degree around the point x = 2

9. Find the Taylor Series for $f(x) = \dfrac{1}{2-x}$ up to 3rd degree around the point x = −1

10. Find the Mclaurin Series for $f(x) = x \cdot e^{2x}$ up to 3rd degree.

11. Find the Mclaurin Series for $f(x) = e^{\sin(x)}$ up to 4th degree.

12. Find the Mclaurin Series for $f(x) = Ln(\sqrt{x+1}+1)$ up to 2nd degree.

13. Find the Mclaurin Series for $f(x) = \dfrac{1}{\sin(x + \dfrac{\pi}{2})}$ up to 2nd degree.

14. Find the Mclaurin Series for $f(x) = \left(Ln(x+1)\right)^2$ up to 3rd degree.

15. Find the Mclaurin Series for $f(x) = e^{\ln(x+1)+1}$, can you explain your answer?

LAGRANGE FORMULA FOR THE ERROR

$$R_n(x) \leq \left| \frac{f^{(n+1)}(c)}{(n+1)!}(x-a)^{n+1} \right|$$, c is a number between a and x that maximizes $f^{(n+1)}$

Example 1: Find the maximum error committed on approximating $\ln(2)$ using the Taylor series of $\ln(x)$ up to 3rd degree around 1.

$$f(x) = \ln(x) \approx (x-1) - \frac{1}{2}(x-1)^2 + \frac{1}{3}(x-1)^3$$

$$f(3) = \ln(3) \approx \frac{8}{3} = 2.666...$$

Error: $R_3(3) = \left| \frac{f^{(4)}(c)}{4!}(3-1)^4 \right|$

Using the 4th derivative of $\ln(x) = f^{(4)} = -\frac{6}{x^4}$

We need to plug into x the value that will <u>maximize</u> it between a = 1 and x = 3, that value is 1, so we use c = 1 which means $f^{(4)}(1) = -\frac{6}{1^4} = -6$. Finally:

$$R_3(3) = \left| \frac{-6}{4!} 2^4 \right| = 4$$

$f(3) = \ln(3) = 2.666... \pm 4$ as can be seen the error committed is even bigger than the value it self.

Example 2: Find the maximum error committed on approximating e^2 using the Taylor series up to 3rd degree around 0 of $f(x) = e^x$

$$f(x) = e^x \approx 1 + x + \frac{1}{2}x^2 + \frac{1}{6}x^2$$

$$f(2) = e^2 \approx \frac{19}{3} = 6.333...$$

Error: $R_3(2) = \left| \frac{f^{(4)}(c)}{4!}(2-0)^4 \right|$

Using the 4th derivative of $e^x = f^{(4)} = e^x$

We need to plug into x the value that will <u>maximize</u> it between a = 0 and x = 2, that value is 2, so we use c = 2 which means $f^{(4)}(2) = e^2$. Finally:

$R_3(3) = \left| \frac{e^2}{4!} 2^4 \right| = \frac{2}{3}e^2$, remembering we are trying to evaluate e^2 indicates an error of up to 66.66..%.

1. Find the value of $\sin(1)$ and maximum error committed on approximating $\sin(1)$ using the Taylor series up to 3rd degree around 0 of $f(x) = \sin(x)$

2. Find the value of $\ln(2)$ and the maximum error committed on approximating $\ln(2)$ using the Taylor series up to 3rd degree around 0 of $f(x) = \ln(x+1)$.

3. Find the value of $\ln(2)$ and the maximum error committed on approximating $\ln(2)$ using the Taylor series up to 2nd degree around 0 of $f(x) = \ln(1+\sin(x))$. What value should be plugged into x?

2.1. – CONTINUITY AND DIFFERENTIABILITY

The function f(x) = |x| has the following aspect:

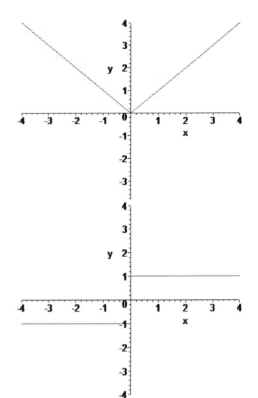

Since we do not know how to differentiate absolute value we write the function as a piecewise function:

$$f(x) = \begin{cases} \underline{\hspace{1cm}}, x < 0 \\ \underline{\hspace{1cm}}, x \geq 0 \end{cases}$$

Now we can differentiate it:

$$f'(x) = \begin{cases} \underline{\hspace{1cm}}, x < 0 \\ \underline{\hspace{1cm}}, x \geq 0 \end{cases}$$

As can be seen the function is continuous at _____ the

derivative however is _____ at _____. This

function is therefore not differentiable at x = 0.

(This statement is not true in general, there might be cases in which the derivative is discontinuous and the function is still differentiable, these functions are beyond the extension of this course).

1. Intuitively, a function that is not "smooth" is not differentiable at a point

   because it's not possible to find a _____ to it at that point.

2. (T/F) a discontinuous function will have a discontinuous derivative.

3. (T/F) a discontinuous derivative will correspond to a discontinuous function.

4. Differentiability is a property of a function at a _____ called a local property.

5. For a function to be differentiable at a point first it **must** be _____ at that point,

6. State the condition for <u>continuity of a function</u> at a point where x = *a*:

7. State the condition for <u>continuity of the derivative</u> at a point where x = *a*:

8. State the **conditions** for <u>differentiability of a function</u> at a point where x = *a*:

9. Fill the table with corresponding graphs of functions:

	f'(x) continuous at c	f'(x) discontinuous at c
f(x) continuous at c	c	c
f(x) discontinuous at c	c	c

10. Given the function:

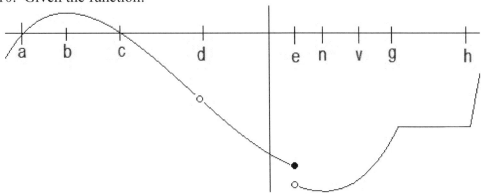

Complete the table:

Fill with:	x	x = a	x = b	x = c	x = d	x = e	x = n	x = v	x = g	x = h
0, + or −	f(x)									
0, + , −, Doesn't exist	f'(x)									
Cont. or Discon.	f(x)									
Cont. or Discon.	f'(x)									
Differ. or Not Differ.	f(x)									

11. There are ____ types of discontinuities:

    I.   _____ Sketch an example:

    II.   _____ Sketch an example:

    III.   _____ Sketch an example:

12. Given $f(x) = x^2$, discuss its continuity and differentiability.

13. Given $f(x) = \dfrac{1}{x-2}$, discuss its continuity and differentiability.

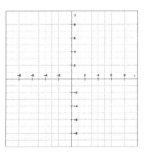

14. Given $f(x) = \dfrac{x-2}{x-2}$, discuss its continuity and differentiability. Sketch it.

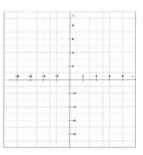

15. Given $f(x) = \dfrac{(x-1)(x+2)}{x+2}$, discuss its continuity and differentiability. Sketch it

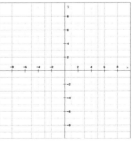

16. Discuss continuity and differentiability of:

$$f(x) = \begin{cases} 2 & x < 2 \\ x & 2 \le x \end{cases}$$

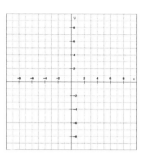

17. Discuss continuity and differentiability of $f(x) = \begin{cases} -x+1 & x < 2 \\ 3 & x = 2 \\ -x+1 & 2 < x \end{cases}$

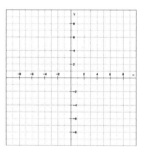

18. Discuss continuity and differentiability of $f(x) = \begin{cases} x^2+1 & x < 1 \\ 2x & 1 \le x \end{cases}$

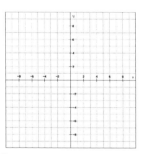

19. Discuss continuity and differentiability of $f(x) = \begin{cases} \ln(x^2) & x < -1 \\ -2x-2 & -1 \le x \end{cases}$

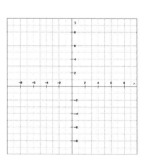

20. Given the following function, discuss its continuity and differentiability.

$$f(x) = \begin{cases} \sqrt{x} & x < 1 \\ 1 & x = 1 \\ \ln(x) + 1 & 1 < x \text{ and } x \leq 3 \\ \dfrac{1}{x-3} & 3 < x \text{ and } x < 5 \\ 3 & x = 5 \\ \dfrac{1}{2} & 5 < x \end{cases}$$

21. Given the following function, find a, and b such that both the function and its derivative will be continuous.

$$f(x) = \begin{cases} a\,x^2 & x < -1 \\ 2\,x^3 + b & -1 \le x \end{cases}$$

22. Given the function, find a, and b such the function is differentiable for any x.

$$f(x) = \begin{cases} a\,x^3 & x < -2 \\ 2\,x^2 - 4\,x + b & -2 \le x \end{cases}$$

23. Write an expression of function that will have the 3 different discontinuities at the points where x = –3, 1 and 5. Sketch the function.

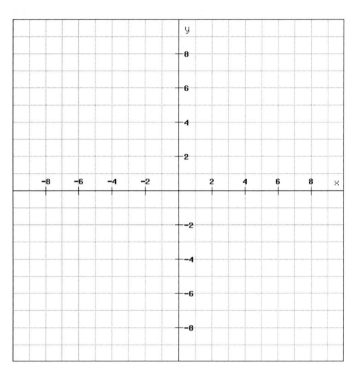

24. Given the following function, find a, b, c and d so that the function is differentiable for any x.

$$f(x) = \begin{cases} 3x - a & x < 1 \\ bx^2 & 1 \leq x \text{ and } x < 4 \\ -cx^2 - 4x + d & 4 \leq x \end{cases}$$

2.2. – ROLLE AND MEAN VALUE THEOREMS

1. **Rolle's Theorem** if $f(x)$ is a continuous on (a, b), differentiable on $[a, b]$ and $f(a) = f(b)$ the there is at least one point in (a, b) with $f'(c) = 0$

2. Graphically it can be seen in the following graph:

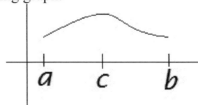

3. In case the function is discontinuous or not differentiable theorem does not hold as can be seen in the following graphs:

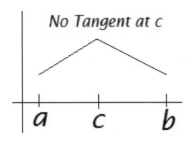 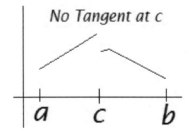

4. Given the function $f(x) = \sin(e^x)$.

   a. Given that $f(x) = \dfrac{1}{2}$, find the x values that solve this equation in $(-1, 1)$

   b. In consequence show that Rolle's Theorem is satisfied by finding the point where the derivative is 0 in this interval.

5. Given the function $f(x) = x^2 \ln(x^2)$.

    a. Given that $f(x) = e$, find all the x value that solve this equation.

    b. In consequence show that the Rolle's Theorem is satisfied by finding the point where the derivative is 0.

6. Given the function $f(x) = |\ln(x)|$.

    a. Given that $f(x) = 2$, find all the x value that solve this equation.

    b. In consequence explain why does Rolle's Theorem is not satisfied in this case.

7. Given the function $f(x) = 5\sin(\frac{5}{x} + \frac{1}{2})$.

    a. Given that $f(x) = 4$, find the 2 biggest solutions for x that solve this equation.

    b. In consequence show that the Rolle's Theorem is satisfied by finding the point where the derivative is 0 between the 2 points found in part a.

8. **The Mean Value Theorem:** if $f(x)$ is a continuous on (a, b), differentiable on $[a, b]$ then there is at least one point in (a, b) with $f'(c) = \dfrac{f(b) - f(a)}{b - a}$

9. Graphically it can be seen in the following graph:

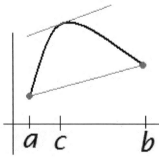

10. In case the function is discontinuous or not differentiable theorem does not hold as can be seen in the following graphs:

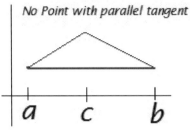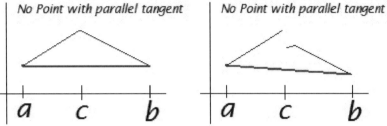

No Point with parallel tangent   No Point with parallel tangent

11. Given the function $f(x) = e^x, x \in [0, \ln(2)]$.

    a. Find the average slope between 0 and ln(2).
    b. Find a point in the same interval in which the tangent will have the same slope to show that the Mean value theorem is true.

12. Given the function $f(x) = \sin(x) + x, x \in [\pi, 2\pi]$.

    a. Find the average slope between π and 2π.

    c. Find a point in the same interval in which the tangent will have this slope to show that the Mean value theorem is true.

13. Given the function $f(x) = \tan(x), x \in [\pi, 2\pi]$.

    a. Find the average slope between π and 2π.

    b. Show that there is no point in the same interval in which the tangent will have this slope, explain why the mean value theorem is not satisfied in this case.

14. Given the function $f(x) = \dfrac{1}{x}, x \in [1, 2]$.

    a. Find the average slope between 1 and 2.

    b. Find a point in the same interval in which the tangent will have this slope.

2.3. – RIEMANN SUMS

1. A Riemann sum is a method to find the area "under" a function. In the following images the lower and upper sum of the function $f(x) = x^2$ between -2 and 2 can be found for different number of intervals:

Number of intervals	Lower Sum	Upper Sum	Difference
5	Sum = 2.56	Sum = 8.83	6.27
10	Sum = 3.84	Sum = 7.04	3.2
50	Sum = 5.02	Sum = 5.66	0.64
500	Sum = 5.30	Sum = 5.37	0.07
5000	Sum = 5.33	Sum = 5.34	0.01

As can be seen as the number of intervals (rectangles) grows the value of the sums becomes similar and approaches the exact value.

2. Approximate the area of the function $f(x) = x$ between 0 and 5 using 5 intervals of corresponding lengths both using the "upper sum" and "lower sum" approximations.

3. Approximate the area of the function $f(x) = \sqrt{x}$ between 1 and 3 using 4 intervals of corresponding lengths both using the "upper sum" and "lower sum" approximations.

4. Approximate the area of the function $f(x) = \dfrac{1}{x}$ between 1 and 4 using 6 intervals of corresponding lengths both using the "upper sum" and "lower sum" approximations.

2.4. – FUNDAMENTAL THEOREM OF CALCULUS

The fundamental theorem of Calculus is usually stated in two parts. The "evaluation part is given by:

If f is continuous on [a, b] and F is any antiderivative of f on [a, b], then

$$\int_a^b f(x)dx = F(b) - F(a)$$

The other part of the theorem can be stated by:

If f is continuous on [a, b], then

$$F(x) = \int_a^x f(t)dt$$

is continuous on [a, b], differentiable on (a, b), and its derivative is

$$F'(x) = \frac{d}{dx}\int_a^x f(t)dt = f(x)$$

Example: In case we want to find the derivative of $F(x) = \int_a^x t^2 dt$, we first execute the integral (**what will be proved as unnecessary**) and then find the derivative.

$$F(x) = \int_a^x t^2 dt = \left[\frac{t^3}{3}\right]_a^x = \frac{x^3}{3} - \frac{a^3}{3} \text{ , } a \text{ is a Real constant.}$$

$$F'(x) = x^2$$

In other words we only needed to plug x into t in the integrand.

Exercises: Find the derivatives of each of the following functions:

1. $F(x) = \int_a^x \sin(t)dt =$

2. $F(x) = \int_a^x t^2 dt =$

3. $F(x) = \displaystyle\int_{2}^{x} \ln(t)\,dt =$

4. $F(x) = \displaystyle\int_{-3}^{x} \arctan(\cos(t)\ln(t^2))\,dt =$

5. $F(x) = \displaystyle\int_{3}^{8} \sin(t)\,dt =$

6. $F(x) = \displaystyle\int_{x}^{8} \sin(t)\,dt =$

7. $F(x) = \displaystyle\int_{x}^{8} e^{3\cos(t)}\,dt =$

8. $F(x) = \displaystyle\int_{0}^{8} \sin^2(t)\,dt =$

Evaluate:

9. $\dfrac{d}{dx} \displaystyle\int_{a}^{x} \dfrac{2}{3t^3 + 4}\,dt =$

10. $\dfrac{d}{dx} \displaystyle\int_{0}^{x} \dfrac{2}{3t^2 + 4}\,dt =$

2.5. – IMPROPER INTEGRALS

1. In occasions we need to evaluate an area that extends to infinity, for examples the are under the curve $f(x) = e^{-x}$ between 0 and infinity:

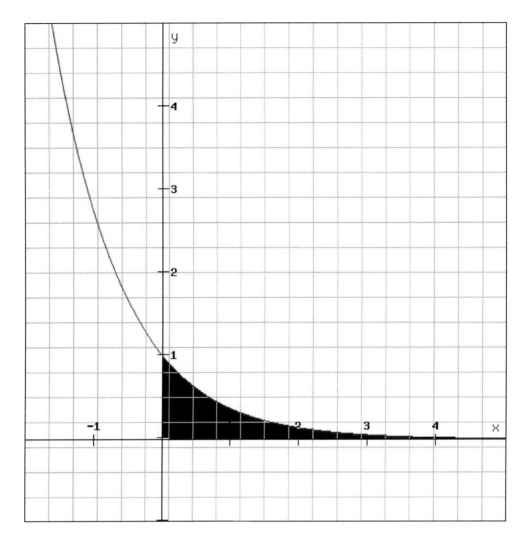

Using definite integration:

$$\int_0^\infty e^{-x}dx = \left[-e^{-x}\right]_0^\infty = \left[Lim_{x\to\infty}(-e^{-x})\right]-\left[-e^{-0}\right]=0+1=1$$

Find the following improper integrals:

2. $\int_2^\infty e^{-x}dx$

3. $\int_0^\infty e^{-0.1x}dx$

4. $\displaystyle\int_{1}^{\infty} \frac{1}{x}dx$

5. $\displaystyle\int_{1}^{\infty} \frac{1}{x^2}dx$

6. $\displaystyle\int_{1}^{\infty} \frac{1}{(2x+3)^4}dx$

7. $\displaystyle\int_{2}^{\infty} \frac{1}{x\sqrt{x}}dx$

8. $\displaystyle\int_{0}^{\infty} e^{-x}dx$

9. $\displaystyle\int_{1}^{\infty} Ln(x)dx$

10. $\displaystyle\int_{3}^{\infty} \frac{\ln(x)}{x^2}dx$

11. $\displaystyle\int_0^\infty \frac{1}{1+x^2}\,dx$

12. $\displaystyle\int_1^\infty \frac{1}{x(1+Ln(x))}\,dx$

13. $\displaystyle\int_1^\infty \frac{1}{x^p}\,dx$

14. $\displaystyle\int_0^\infty xe^{-x}\,dx$

15. $\displaystyle\int_0^\infty x^2 e^{-x}\,dx$

16. $\displaystyle\int_0^\infty x^n e^{-x}\,dx$

3.1. – INTRODUCTION TO DIFFERENTIAL EQUATIONS

1. A differential equation is an equation that relates a function with its _____.

2. For example, the derivative of $f(x) = e^x + C$ is $f'(x) = \dfrac{df}{dx} = e^x$. The corresponding differential equation is $f(x) = \dfrac{df}{dx} = f'(x) = e^x$. Writing the same equation using y instead of f gives:

$$\frac{dy}{dx} = e^x$$

   Now can separate to "x" and "y": $dy = e^x dx$

   Integrating both sides gives: $y = e^x + C$ which is the expected result.

3. Given the function $f(x) = e^{-x}$. Write a corresponding differential equation that will relate the function with its derivative.

4. Verify that $f(x) = \dfrac{a}{1 + \ln(x)} + C$ is a solution of $f'(x) = -x(\ln(x) + 1)f(x)$

5. Given the function $f(x) = \sin(x)$. Write a differential corresponding equation that will relate the function with its 2nd derivative.

6. Given the function $f(x) = \dfrac{1}{x}$. Write a differential corresponding equation that will relate the function with its 1st derivative. Part of the solution is: $f(x) = f'(x) \cdot$ ____

3.2. – SLOPE FIELDS

1. Given the following differential equation $f'(x) = \dfrac{df}{dx} = x - y$. This means that the value of the slope of the tangent to the curve is the sum of the coordinates of the point. For example at the point (2, 2) the value of the slope is _____. At the point (0, 2) the value of the slope is _____ etc. This allows us to graph the family of curves that form the solution by sketching a "little slope" at the sufficiently large number of points:

The solution of the diferential equation is any of the curves produced (one is sketched as an example)

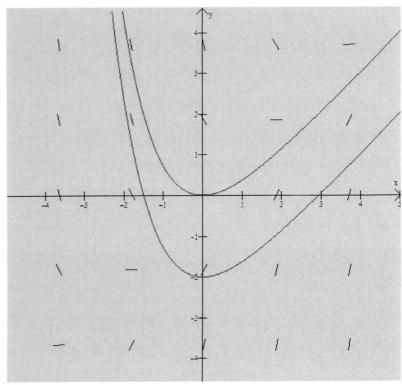

An **Isocline** is a line on which the slope of the curve is constant, for example 3 are sketched for the previous example:

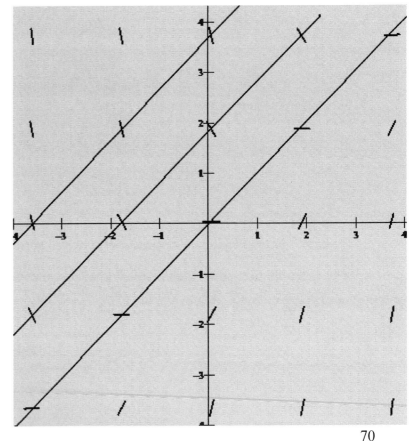

Draw the slope field that corresponds to each one of the differential equations, add one curve and one isocline to your sketch.

2. $\dfrac{df}{dx} = y$

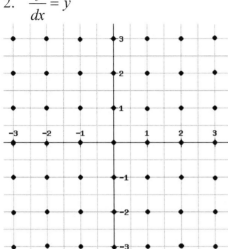

5. $\dfrac{df}{dx} = \dfrac{y}{x}$

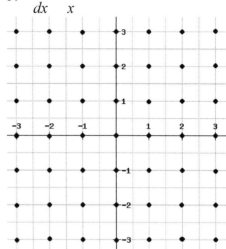

3. $\dfrac{df}{dx} = x^2$

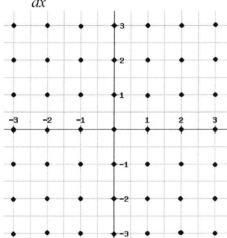

6. $\dfrac{df}{dx} = 2 - y$

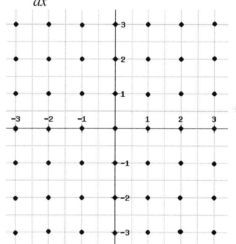

4. $\dfrac{df}{dx} = y + x$

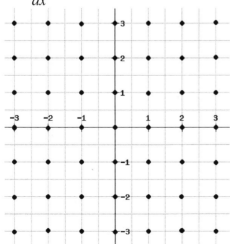

7. $\dfrac{df}{dx} = x^2 + y$

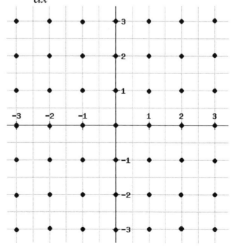

8. $\dfrac{df}{dx} = 2^x$

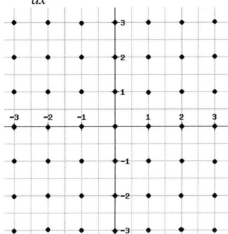

11. $\dfrac{df}{dx} = \sin(x)$

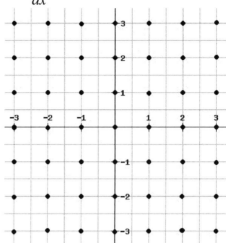

9. $\dfrac{df}{dx} = x^2 + y^2$

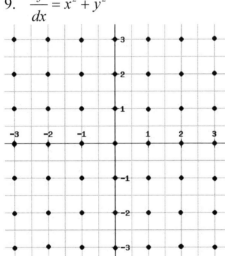

12. $\dfrac{df}{dx} = \ln(x)$

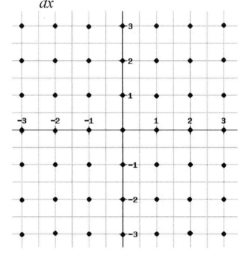

10. $\dfrac{df}{dx} = \dfrac{1}{y}$

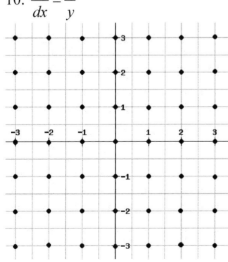

13. $\dfrac{df}{dx} = \tan(x)$

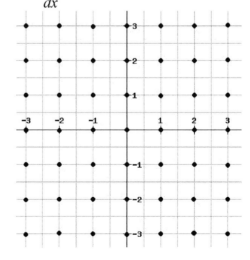

3.3. – EULER'S METHOD

1. Leonard Euler has developed a method to solve differential equations numerically by approximation to the solution. $y_{n+1} = y_n + h \cdot f(x_n, y_n); x_{n+1} = x_n + h$ where h is the step length and $f(x_n, y_n)$ is the value of the derivative at the point (x_n, y_n)

2. **For example:** Solve the following differential equation $\dfrac{dy}{dx} = x - e^y$ using Euler's method with initial conditions x = 0, y = 0. Use 5 steps to estimate the value of y at x = 0.5.

   Since x is between 0 and 0.5 and 5 steps are requested the size of each step is 0.1. We use the following table:

Step number	0	1	2	3	4	5
x	0	0.1	0.2	0.3	0.4	0.5
y	0	$y_{n+1} = 0 + 0.1(-1) = -0.1$	−0.1805	−0.2440	−0.2923	−0.3270
$f(x_n, y_n)$	$f(x_n, y_n) = 0 - e^0 = -1$	$f(x_n, y_n) \approx -0.804$				

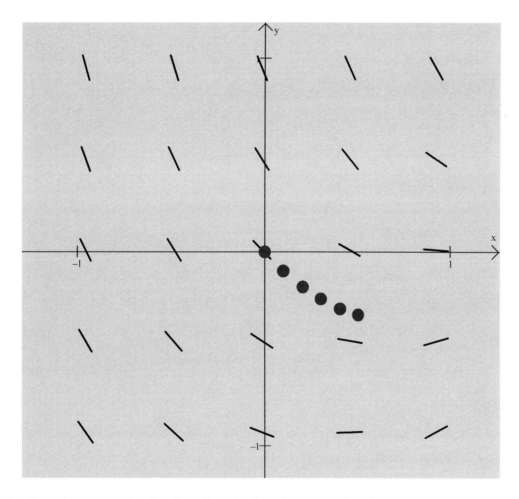

The 6 points shown are the 6 points found using the approximation.
3.

4. Solve the following differential equation $\frac{dy}{dx} = x^2 + y$ using Euler's method with initial conditions x = 0, y = 1. Use 5 steps to estimate the value of y at x = 0.5.

Step number	0	1	2	3	4	5
x						
y						
$\frac{df}{dx}$						

5. Solve the following differential equation $\frac{df}{dx} = \ln(x^2) - y^2$ using Euler's method with initial conditions x = −1, y = 0. Use 4 steps to estimate the value of y at x = −0.2.

Step number	0	1	2	3	4
x					
y					
$\frac{df}{dx}$					

6. Solve the following differential equation $\dfrac{df}{dx} = \dfrac{1}{x} + y$ using Euler's method with initial conditions x = 1, y = 1. Use 5 steps to estimate the value of y at x = 2.

Step number	0	1	2	3	4	5
x						
y						
$\dfrac{df}{dx}$						

7. Solve the following differential equation $\dfrac{df}{dx} = \dfrac{y}{x+y}$ using Euler's method with initial conditions x = 0, y = 1. Use 5 steps to estimate the value of y at x = 0.5.

Step number	0	1	2	3	4	5
x						
y						
$\dfrac{df}{dx}$						

3.4. – SEPERABLE DIFFERENTIAL EQUATIONS

1. A separable differential equation is an equation like the one seen the previous part, where the parts in "x" and "y" can be separated and integration take place on both sides of the equation.

    For example: $\dfrac{dy}{dx} = x + e^x$

    Now can separate to "x" and "y": $dy = (x + e^x)dx$

    Integrating both sides gives: $\displaystyle\int dy = \int (x + e^x)dx$

    $$y = \dfrac{x^2}{2} + e^x + C .$$

Solve the differential equations that are separable, if possible express y in terms of x:

2. $\dfrac{dy}{dx} = 1$

3. $\dfrac{dy}{dx} = 2xy$

4. $\dfrac{dy}{dx} = \dfrac{x+y}{y}$

5. $\dfrac{dy}{dx} = \dfrac{x}{y}$

6. $\dfrac{dy}{dx} = x + \ln(y)$

7. $\dfrac{1}{x} \cdot \dfrac{dy}{dx} = y \cdot e^x$

8. $(1 + x^2)\dfrac{dy}{dx} = y$

9. $\dfrac{dy}{dx} = xy + \dfrac{x}{y}$

10. $\dfrac{dy}{dx} = \dfrac{e^{2x}+1}{y^2}$

11. $\dfrac{dy}{dx} = \dfrac{1}{\sin(y)\sqrt{1-x^2}}$

12. $\dfrac{dy}{dx} = \dfrac{xe^{2xy}}{2}$

13. $\dfrac{dy}{dx} = e^{2x+y}$

14. $\dfrac{dy}{dx} = x\tan(y)$

15. $\dfrac{dy}{dx} = xy^2$

16. $\dfrac{dy}{dx} = \dfrac{\sec(y)}{y(3x+4)}$

17. $\dfrac{dy}{dx} = x + y$

3.5. – HOMOGENEOUS DIFFERENTIAL EQUATIONS

1. A homogeneous differential equation is one that can be reduced to a separable by doing the change of variable $v = \dfrac{y}{x}$

    For example: $\dfrac{dy}{dx} = \dfrac{x+y}{x}$ can be rewritten: $\dfrac{dy}{dx} = \left(1 + \dfrac{y}{x}\right)$

    Switching $v = \dfrac{y}{x}$ gives $1 + v$ on RHS

    But, since $y = vx$ and therefore: $\dfrac{dy}{dx} = v + x\dfrac{dv}{dx}$ (which is the LHS), finally:

    $v + x\dfrac{dv}{dx} = 1 + v$,   Now can separate to "x" and "v":

    $dv = \dfrac{dx}{x}$ Integrating both sides gives:

    $v = \ln(x) + c$ Undo the switch:

    $\dfrac{y}{x} = \ln(x) + c$

    $y = x(\ln(x) + c)$ The final result

2. Solve the following equation by separating the variables and also using the change $v = \dfrac{y}{x}$.

    $\dfrac{dy}{dx} = \dfrac{y}{x}$

Solve the following equations (Separable or homogeneous), if possible express y in terms of x or alternatively x in terms of y.

3. $\dfrac{dy}{dx} = \dfrac{y^2 + xy}{x^2}$

4. $\dfrac{dy}{dx} = \dfrac{y}{x + y}$

5. $\dfrac{dy}{dx} = xy + \dfrac{x}{y}$

6. $\dfrac{dy}{dx} = \dfrac{y^2 + x^2 + xy}{x^2}$

7. $\dfrac{dy}{dx} = e^{2x+y}$

8. $\dfrac{dy}{dx} = \dfrac{y^2 + x^2 - xy}{x^2}$

9. $\dfrac{dy}{dx} = \dfrac{e^{2x} + 1}{y^2}$

10. $\dfrac{dy}{dx} = \dfrac{y}{x} + e^{\frac{y}{x}}$

11. $\dfrac{dy}{dx} = \dfrac{1}{\sin(y)\sqrt{1-x^2}}$

12. $\dfrac{dy}{dx} = \dfrac{yxe^{2x}}{2}$

13. $\dfrac{dy}{dx} = \dfrac{x^2 y + 6y^3}{x^3 + y^2 x}$

14. $\dfrac{dy}{dx} = x\tan(y)$

15. $\dfrac{dy}{dx} = \ln(x)y^2$

16. $\dfrac{dy}{dx} = \dfrac{\sec(y)}{y(3x+4)}$

3.6. – INTEGRATING FACTOR

1. Differential equations that have the form:

$$y' + M(x)y = Q(x)$$

May be solved using what is called an "integrating factor". M(x) and Q(x) are any continuous functions of x.

2. The idea behind is that we **multiply both sides** of the equation by this factor, $U(x)$, the left side of the equation becomes **the derivative of** $y \cdot U(x)$:

$$U(x)\big(y' + M(x)y\big) = Q(x) \cdot U(x)$$

$$\big(U(x) \cdot y\big)' = Q(x) \cdot U(x)$$

Then we integrate: $\qquad U(x) \cdot y = \int Q(x) \cdot U(x)dx$

The "secret" is What is $U(x)$? Without proving it $U(x) = e^{\int M(x)dx}$

Example: Solve $y' = x + y$, first check it follows the structure: $y' + M(x)y = Q(x)$

It does: $\qquad y' - y = x \qquad M(x) = -1 \qquad Q(x) = x$

So $\qquad U(x) = e^{\int M(x)dx} = e^{\int -1 dx} = e^{-x}$

Multiply both sides by e^{-x} $\qquad e^{-x}y' - e^{-x}y = e^{-x}x$

Gives: $\qquad (e^{-x}y)' = e^{-x}x$

Integrating both sides $\qquad e^{-x}y = -e^{-x}(1+x) + C$

Finally: $\qquad y = \dfrac{-e^{-x}(1+x) + C}{e^{-x}}$

3. Solve the following differential equations using an integrating factor and then by separation of variables, make sure the same result is obtained.

$$y' + xy = x$$

Solve the following differential equations using an integrating factor:

4. $y' + y = e^x$

5. $y' = \sin(2x) - y$

6. $y' + \dfrac{y}{x} = x^2$

7. $y' + y = x \cdot e^x$

8. $x\dfrac{dy}{dx} = \dfrac{1}{x} - y$

9. $xy' + 2y = \dfrac{1}{x^2}$

10. $\dfrac{dy}{dx} = \sin(x) - + \dfrac{y}{x}$

11. $y' + \dfrac{2y}{x} = e^x$

12. $\dfrac{dy}{dx} + \dfrac{y}{\sqrt{x}} = 1$

13. $y' + \dfrac{2y}{x} = \ln(x)$

14. $\sqrt{x}\,y' + 2y = x\sqrt{x}$

1.1. – LIMITS

ANSWER KEY

Introduction:

1. $x \to \infty$ means that <u>x is a very large positive number in context of the problem</u>
2. $x \to -\infty$ means that <u>x is a very large negative number in context of the problem</u>
3. $x \to 3$ means that <u>x is a number close to 3 on either side,</u> **not** 3 itself.
4. $x \to 3^+$ means that <u>x is a number a bit bigger than 3</u> **not** 3 itself.
5. $x \to 3^-$ means that <u>x is a number a bit smaller than 3</u> **not** 3 itself.
6. $x \to 0^-$ means that <u>x is a number a bit smaller than 0 so a negative number.</u>
7. $x \to 0^+$ means that <u>x is a number a bit bigger than 0 so a positive number.</u>

8. $Lim\left(\dfrac{0}{\infty}\right) =$

9. $Lim\left(\dfrac{\infty}{0}\right) = D.E.(\pm\infty)$

10. $Lim\left(\dfrac{2}{3}\right) = \dfrac{2}{3}$

11. $Lim\left(\dfrac{0^+}{\infty}\right) = 0$

12. $Lim\left(\dfrac{0^+}{-\infty}\right) = 0$

13. $Lim\left(\dfrac{-\infty}{0^-}\right) = \infty$

14. $Lim\left(\dfrac{\infty}{\infty}\right) = $ undetermined

15. $Lim\left(\dfrac{0}{0}\right) = $ undetermined

16. $Lim(1^\infty) = $ undetermined

17. $Lim(\infty^1) = \infty$

18. $Lim(\infty^0) = $ undetermined

19. $Lim\left(\dfrac{1}{\infty}\right) = 0$

20. $Lim(\infty - \infty) = $ undetermined

21. $Lim(\infty + \infty) = \infty$

22. $Lim(0 - 0) = 0$

23. $Lim(2 - \infty) = -\infty$

24. $Lim(0 - 5) = -5$

25. $Lim(\infty^{-1}) = 0$

GRAPHICAL INTERPRETATION OF LIMITS

1. Given the graph of the function:

   a. $\lim\limits_{x\to 0^-}(f(x)) = 1$ $\quad \lim\limits_{x\to 0^+}(f(x)) = 1$ $\qquad f(0) = 1$ $\qquad \lim\limits_{x\to 0}(f(x)) = 1$

   b. Since $\lim\limits_{x\to 0^-}(f(x)) = \lim\limits_{x\to 0^+}(f(x)) = f(0)$ the function is <u>continuous</u> at x = 0.

   c. $\lim\limits_{x\to -3^+}(f(x)) = 0.5$ $\quad \lim\limits_{x\to -3^-}(f(x)) = 0.5$ $\qquad f(3) = 0.5$ $\qquad \lim\limits_{x\to -3}(f(x)) = 0.5$

   d. Since $\lim\limits_{x\to -3^-}(f(x)) = \lim\limits_{x\to -3^+}(f(x)) = f(-3)$ the function is <u>continuous</u> at x = −3.

   e. $\lim\limits_{x\to -2^+}(f(x)) = 8$ $\quad \lim\limits_{x\to -2^-}(f(x)) = -\infty$ $\qquad f(-2) = D.E.$ $\quad \lim\limits_{x\to -2}(f(x)) = D.E.$

   f. Since $\lim\limits_{x\to -2^-}(f(x)) \neq \lim\limits_{x\to -2^+}(f(x))$ and <u>$f(-2)$ does not exist</u> the function
      has an <u>infinite jump discontinuity</u> at x= −2.

   g. $\lim\limits_{x\to 1^-}(f(x)) = 2$ $\quad \lim\limits_{x\to 1^+}(f(x)) = 4$ $\qquad f(1) = 6$ $\qquad \lim\limits_{x\to 1}(f(x)) = D.E.$

   h. Since $\lim\limits_{x\to 1^-}(f(x)) \neq \lim\limits_{x\to 1^+}(f(x))$ and $f(1) = 6$ the function has <u>a finite jump</u>
      <u>discontinuity</u> at x = 1

   i. $\lim\limits_{x\to 2^+}(f(x)) = 4$ $\quad \lim\limits_{x\to 2^-}(f(x)) = 4$ $\qquad f(2) = 2$ $\qquad \lim\limits_{x\to 2}(f(x)) = 4$

j. Since $\lim\limits_{x\to2^-}(f(x)) = \lim\limits_{x\to2^+}(f(x))$ and $f(2) = 2$ the function has <u>a removable</u> <u>discontinuity</u> at x = 2.

k. Using the graph find all the values of a for which f(a) does not exist: <u>a = 3</u>

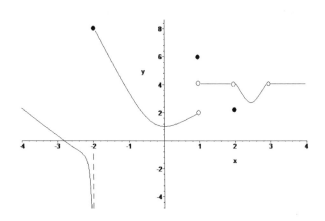

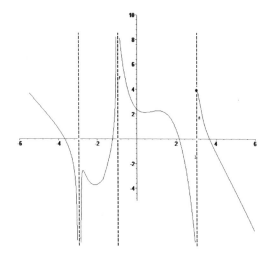

2. Given the graph of the function:

a. $\lim\limits_{x\to0^-}(f(x)) = 2.4$

b. $\lim\limits_{x\to0^+}(f(x)) = 2.4$

c. $\lim\limits_{x\to0}(f(x)) = 2.4$

d. $\lim\limits_{x\to-3^+}(f(x)) = -\infty$

e. $\lim\limits_{x\to-3^-}(f(x)) = -\infty$

f. $\lim\limits_{x\to-3}(f(x)) = -\infty$

g. $f(-3) = D.E.$

h. $\lim\limits_{x\to3^+}(f(x)) = 4$

i. $\lim\limits_{x\to3^-}(f(x)) = -\infty$

j. $\lim\limits_{x\to3}(f(x)) = D.E.$

k. $f(3) = 4$

l. $\lim\limits_{x\to-1^-}(f(x)) = \infty$

m. $\lim\limits_{x\to-1^+}(f(x)) = \infty$

n. $\lim\limits_{x\to-1}(f(x)) = \infty$

o. $f(-1) = D.E.$

l. State the equations of all the asymptotes: $x = -3, x = -1, x = 3$

m. State all the points with discontinuities and the kind of discontinuity.

  At $x = -3$ inifinite jump

  At $x = -1$ inifinite jump

  At $x = 3$ inifinite jump

3. Find the following <u>limits</u>:

$\lim\limits_{x\to\infty}(f(x)) = 2$

$\lim\limits_{x\to\infty}(f(x)) = D.E.$

$\lim\limits_{x\to\infty}(f(x)) = 3$

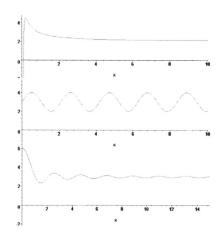

4. Find the limits:

$$\lim_{x \to \infty}(f(x)) = 0$$

$$\lim_{x \to -\infty}(f(x)) = D.E.$$

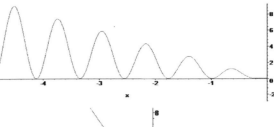

$$\lim_{x \to -\infty}(f(x)) = \infty$$

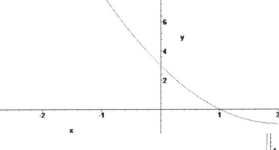

$$\lim_{x \to -\infty}(f(x)) = -3$$

5. Horizontal asymptotes appear for <u>large positive or negative of x</u>, in case we look for them we need to check the limit of the function when x tends to <u>infinity</u> or <u>negative infinity</u>
6. Vertical asymptotes appear for <u>a certain value</u> of x We check lateral limits to see the behaviour of the function next to it.

THE "SQUEEZE" THEOREM

If we know that the value of a certain function f for a certain value of x satisfies $p(a) = M \le f(a) \le q(a) = N$ it means $M \le f(a) \le N$.

For example: in case we want to find the limit $Lim_{x \to \infty}(\dfrac{e^{\sin(x)}}{x})$

$e^{-1} \le e^{\sin(x)} \le e^{1}$, divide both sides by x gives

$Lim_{x \to \infty}\left(\dfrac{e^{-1}}{x}\right) = 0 \le Lim_{x \to \infty}\left(\dfrac{e^{\sin(x)}}{x}\right) \le Lim_{x \to \infty}\left(\dfrac{e^{1}}{x}\right) = 0$ therefore $Lim_{x \to \infty}(\dfrac{e^{\sin(x)}}{x}) = 0$

LIMITS TYPE $x \to \pm\infty$

1. $\lim\limits_{x \to \infty}\left(\dfrac{2x}{x}\right) = 2$

2. $\lim\limits_{x \to \infty}\left(\dfrac{2x}{x^2}\right) = 0$

3. $\lim\limits_{x \to \infty}\left(\dfrac{2x^2}{x}\right) = \infty$

4. $\lim\limits_{x \to \infty}\left(\dfrac{2x}{x+1}\right) = 2$

5. $\lim\limits_{x \to \infty}\left(\dfrac{x}{2x+10}\right) = \dfrac{1}{2}$

6. $\lim\limits_{x \to \infty}\left(\dfrac{2x}{3x+1}\right) = \dfrac{2}{3}$

7. $\lim\limits_{x \to \infty}\left(\dfrac{2x^2}{6x^3-22}\right) = 0$

8. $\lim\limits_{x \to \infty}\left(\dfrac{3x^2+1}{2x-2}\right) = \infty$

92

9. $\lim\limits_{x\to-\infty}\left(\dfrac{2x^2+1}{5x^2-2}\right)=\dfrac{2}{5}$

10. $\lim\limits_{x\to\infty}\left(\dfrac{ax^2+1}{bx-2}\right)=sign(\dfrac{a}{b})\cdot\infty$

11. $\lim\limits_{x\to-\infty}\left(\dfrac{ax^3+4x}{bx^4+5x^2-2}\right)=0$

12. $=\lim\limits_{x\to-\infty}\left(\dfrac{ax^7+4x}{bx^7+7x^2-x}\right)=\dfrac{a}{b}$

13. $\lim\limits_{x\to-\infty}\left(\dfrac{\sqrt{3}x^7+4x}{-2x^7+7x^2-x}\right)=\dfrac{\sqrt{3}}{-2}$

14. $\lim\limits_{x\to-\infty}\left(\dfrac{-2x^5+4x^2+4}{x^3+81x^2-2x}\right)=-\infty$

15. $\lim\limits_{x\to-\infty}\left(\dfrac{1}{6}\dfrac{\sqrt{35}(2x^4+4x^2+4)}{2x^4+81x^2-2x}\right)=\dfrac{\sqrt{35}}{6}$

16. $\lim\limits_{x\to\infty}\left(\dfrac{(x+5)^4}{(2x-4)^4}\right)=\dfrac{1}{16}$

17. $\lim\limits_{x\to-\infty}\left(\dfrac{(4x+1)^5}{(2x-7)^5}\right)=32$

18. $\lim\limits_{x\to-\infty}\left(\dfrac{(5x^2+2)^5}{(2x-3)^6}\right)=\infty$

19. $\lim\limits_{x\to\infty}\left(\dfrac{(5x^2+2)(x+3)}{(2x-3)(x^2+1)}\right)=\dfrac{5}{2}$

20. $\lim\limits_{x\to-\infty}\left(\dfrac{(x+2)(2x+3)}{(5x-3)(2x^2+4)}\right)=0$

21. $\lim\limits_{x\to\infty}\left(\dfrac{\sqrt{x^5+7x}}{x^2\sqrt{2x}}\right)=\dfrac{1}{\sqrt{2}}$

22. $\lim\limits_{x\to\infty}\left(\dfrac{\sqrt{3x^4-x}}{x\sqrt{5x^3}}\right)=0$

23. $\lim\limits_{x\to-\infty}\left(\dfrac{\sqrt{32x^4-3x+5}}{3x^2}\right)=\dfrac{\sqrt{32}}{3}$

24. $\lim\limits_{x\to-\infty}\left(\dfrac{x+\sqrt{2x^2-3}}{7x+1}\right)=\dfrac{1+\sqrt{2}}{7}$

25. $\lim\limits_{x\to-\infty}\left(\dfrac{2x^2+\sqrt{2x^4-3}}{-7x^2+1}\right)=\dfrac{2+\sqrt{2}}{-7}$

$\lim\limits_{x\to\infty}\left(\dfrac{ax^n+bx^{n-1}+...}{kx^m+sx^{m-1}+...}\right)=$

26. $if\quad n>m\quad sign(\dfrac{a}{k})\cdot\infty$

$\quad if\quad n=m\quad \dfrac{a}{k}$

$\quad if\quad n<m\quad 0$

27. $\lim\limits_{x\to\infty}\left(\dfrac{x^{40}}{2^x}\right)=0$

28. $\lim\limits_{x\to\infty}\left(\dfrac{2^x}{8x^{50}}\right)=\infty$

29. $\lim\limits_{x\to-\infty}\left(\dfrac{x^{400}}{-3^x}\right)=-\infty$

30. $\lim\limits_{x\to\infty}\left(\dfrac{\sqrt{x^3-x}}{\sqrt{x^2-2x}}\right)=\infty$

31. $\lim\limits_{x\to\infty}\left(\dfrac{\sqrt{x^3+x}}{\sqrt{2x^3-2x}}\right)=\dfrac{1}{\sqrt{2}}$

32. $\lim\limits_{x\to-\infty}(2^x-x^{12})=-\infty$

33. $\lim\limits_{x\to\infty}(2^x-x^{12})=\infty$

34. $\lim\limits_{x\to\infty}(\sqrt{x^3-x+2}-x+3)=\infty$

35. $\lim\limits_{x\to\infty}(3^x-2^x)=\infty$

36. $\lim\limits_{x\to-\infty}(3^x-2^x)=0$

37. $\lim\limits_{x\to\infty}(\sqrt{x}-\ln(x))=\infty$

38. $\lim\limits_{x\to\infty}(e^x-\ln(x))=\infty$

39. $\lim\limits_{x\to\infty}\left(\dfrac{6^x}{5^x}\right)=\infty$

40. $\lim\limits_{x\to\infty}\left(\dfrac{8^x}{9^x}\right)=0$

41. $\lim\limits_{x\to\infty}\left(\left(\dfrac{188}{189}\right)^x\right)=0$

$\lim\limits_{x\to\infty}\left(\left(\dfrac{a}{b}\right)^x\right)=$

42. $if\quad a>b\quad \infty$

$\quad f\quad a=b\quad 1$

$\quad f\quad a<b\quad 0$

43. $\lim\limits_{x \to \infty}\left(\dfrac{6^x - 4^x}{5^x + 5^{-x}}\right) = \infty$

49. $\lim\limits_{x \to \infty}\left(\cos\left(\dfrac{1}{x}\right)\right) = 1$

44. $\lim\limits_{x \to -\infty}\left(\dfrac{6^x - 4^x}{5^x + 5^{-x}}\right) = 0$

50. $\lim\limits_{x \to \infty}\left(\dfrac{1}{\cos(x)}\right) = D.E.$

45. $\lim\limits_{x \to \infty}\left(\dfrac{x^5 + x + 2}{e^x}\right) = 0$

51. $\lim\limits_{x \to \infty}\left(\dfrac{1}{\ln(x)}\right) = 0$

46. $\lim\limits_{x \to \infty}(\sqrt{x^2 - x + 2} - x^{1.1} + 3) = -\infty$

52. $\lim\limits_{x \to \infty}(\ln(x) - \ln(2x)) = \ln\left(\dfrac{1}{2}\right)$

47. $\lim\limits_{x \to \infty}(\sin(x)) = D.E.$

48. $\lim\limits_{x \to \infty}\left(\dfrac{\sin(x)}{x}\right) = 0$

53.
$$\lim\limits_{x \to \infty}(x - \sqrt{x^2 - 2x + 5}) = \lim\limits_{x \to \infty}(x - \sqrt{x^2 - 2x + 5})\dfrac{(x + \sqrt{x^2 - 2x + 5})}{(x + \sqrt{x^2 - 2x + 5})} =$$
$$\lim\limits_{x \to \infty}\dfrac{2x - 5}{(x + \sqrt{x^2 - 2x + 5})} = 1$$

54.
$$\lim\limits_{x \to \infty}\left(\dfrac{\sqrt{x^4 + 2x^3 - 3} - \sqrt{x^4 - x}}{x + 5}\right) = \lim\limits_{x \to \infty}\left(\dfrac{\sqrt{x^4 + 2x^3 - 3} - \sqrt{x^4 - x}}{x + 5}\right)\left(\dfrac{\sqrt{x^4 + 2x^3 - 3} + \sqrt{x^4 - x}}{\sqrt{x^4 + 2x^3 - 3} + \sqrt{x^4 - x}}\right) =$$
$$\lim\limits_{x \to \infty}\left(\dfrac{1}{x + 5}\right)\left(\dfrac{2x^3 - 3 + x}{\sqrt{x^4 + 2x^3 - 3} + \sqrt{x^4 - x}}\right) = 1$$

55.
$$\lim\limits_{x \to \infty}(\sqrt{x^2 + x} - \sqrt{x^2 - x}) = \lim\limits_{x \to \infty}(\sqrt{x^2 + x} - \sqrt{x^2 - x})\dfrac{(\sqrt{x^2 + x} + \sqrt{x^2 - x})}{(\sqrt{x^2 + x} + \sqrt{x^2 - x})} =$$
$$\lim\limits_{x \to \infty}\dfrac{2x}{(\sqrt{x^2 + x} + \sqrt{x^2 - x})} = 1$$

56.
$$\lim\limits_{x \to \infty}(\sqrt{x^2 + x} - \sqrt{x^2 - ax}) = \lim\limits_{x \to \infty}(\sqrt{x^2 + x} - \sqrt{x^2 - ax})\dfrac{\sqrt{x^2 + x} + \sqrt{x^2 - ax}}{\sqrt{x^2 + x} + \sqrt{x^2 - ax}} =$$
$$\lim\limits_{x \to \infty}\dfrac{x(1 + a)}{\sqrt{x^2 + x} + \sqrt{x^2 - ax}} = \dfrac{1 + a}{2}$$

57. $\lim\limits_{x \to \infty}(\sqrt{x^3 + x} - \sqrt{x^2 - 2x}) = \infty$

LIMITS TYPE $x \to a$

Properties of limits

Fill the missing blanks:

a. $\lim_{x \to a}(c) = c, c \in R$

b. $\lim_{x \to a}(x) = a$

c. $\lim_{x \to a}(f(x) + g(x)) = \lim_{x \to a}(f(x)) + \lim_{x \to a}(g(x))$, the limit of the sum is the sum of the limits.

d. $\lim_{x \to a}(c(f(x))) = c \lim_{x \to a}(f(x)), c \in R$, constants can be taken out of the limit.

e. $\lim_{x \to a}(f(x) \cdot g(x)) = \lim_{x \to a}(f(x)) \cdot \lim_{x \to a}(g(x))$, the limit of the product is the product of the limits.

f. $\lim_{x \to a}\left(\dfrac{f(x)}{g(x)}\right) = \dfrac{\lim_{x \to a}(f(x))}{\lim_{x \to a}(g(x))}, \lim_{x \to a}(g(x)) \neq 0$, the limit of the quotient is the quotient of the limits.

g. $\lim_{x \to a}((f(x))^n) = (\lim_{x \to a}(f(x)))^n, n \in R$

Exercises

Compute the following limits and indicate which properties are being used:

58. $\lim_{x \to 2}((x^2 + 5)(x - 3)) = -9$

59. $\lim_{x \to 2}((x^3 - \ln(x - 1)) + (2^x + x - 3)) = 11$

60. $\lim_{x \to 3}\left(\dfrac{(3x^2 - 5)x}{x^3 - 4}\right) = \dfrac{66}{23}$

61. $\lim_{x \to 1}\left(\left(\left(2x + \cos(\pi x)\right)^{10}\right)\right) = 1$

The following limits are given:

$$\lim_{x \to 4}(f(x)) = 3, \lim_{x \to 4}(g(x)) = -2, \lim_{x \to 4}(h(x)) = \dfrac{2}{5}$$

Compute the following limits:

62. $\lim_{x \to 4}(3f(x) + 4g(x)) = 1$

63. $\lim_{x \to 4}(f(x) - 2g(x) - h(x)) = 7 - \dfrac{2}{5} = \dfrac{33}{5}$

64. $\lim_{x \to 4}(\sqrt{(f(x))^2 + (g(x))^4}) = \sqrt{(3)^2 + (-2)^4} = 5$

Find the following limit:

65. $\lim_{x \to 5}\left(\dfrac{x^2 - 8x + 15}{x - 5}\right) = \dfrac{0}{0}$

As you can see if we substitute x = 5 we obtain a fraction of the form $\dfrac{0}{0}$, therefore we must simplify:

$$\lim_{x \to 5}\left(\dfrac{x^2 - 8x + 15}{x - 5}\right) = \lim_{x \to 5}\left(\dfrac{(x - 5)(x - 3)}{x - 5}\right) = \lim_{x \to 5}(x - 3) = 2$$

66. $\lim\limits_{x \to -2}\left(\dfrac{x^2 - x - 6}{x + 2}\right) = \dfrac{0}{0} = \lim\limits_{x \to -2}\left(\dfrac{(x+2)(x-3)}{x+2}\right) = -5$

67. $\lim\limits_{x \to -1}\left(\dfrac{3x^3 + 5x^2 + 3x}{1 + x}\right) = \dfrac{-1}{0} = D.E.(\pm\infty)$

68. $\lim\limits_{x \to -2}\left(\dfrac{-4x - 8}{2 + x}\right) = \dfrac{0}{0} = \lim\limits_{x \to -2}\left(\dfrac{-4(x+2)}{2+x}\right) = -4 =$

69. $\lim\limits_{x \to -2}\left(\dfrac{x^3 + 8}{x^2 - 4}\right) = \dfrac{0}{0} = \lim\limits_{x \to -2}\left(\dfrac{(x+2)(x^2 - 2x + 4)}{(x-2)(x+2)}\right) = \dfrac{12}{-4} = -3$

70. $\lim\limits_{x \to 2}\left(\dfrac{-2x^4 + 1}{5x^3 - 2}\right) = \dfrac{-31}{38}$

71.
$\lim\limits_{t \to 0}\left(\dfrac{\sqrt{3-t} - \sqrt{3}}{t}\right) = \dfrac{0}{0} = \lim\limits_{t \to 0}\left(\dfrac{\sqrt{3-t} - \sqrt{3}}{t}\right)\left(\dfrac{\sqrt{3-t} + \sqrt{3}}{\sqrt{3-t} + \sqrt{3}}\right) =$

$\lim\limits_{t \to 0}\left(\dfrac{1}{t}\right)\left(\dfrac{-t}{\sqrt{3-t} + \sqrt{3}}\right) = \dfrac{-1}{2\sqrt{3}}$

72. $\lim\limits_{h \to 0}\left(\dfrac{(h+2)^3 - 8}{h}\right) = \dfrac{0}{0} = \lim\limits_{h \to 0}\left(\dfrac{h^3 + 6h^2 + 6h}{h}\right) = \lim\limits_{h \to 0}\left(h^2 + 6h + 6\right) = 6$

73. $\lim\limits_{x \to 1}\left(\dfrac{1}{x-1} - \dfrac{2}{x^2 - 1}\right) = \lim\limits_{x \to 1}\left(\dfrac{x-1}{x^2-1}\right) = \lim\limits_{x \to 1}\left(\dfrac{1}{x+1}\right) = \dfrac{1}{2}$

74. $\lim\limits_{x \to 2}\left(\dfrac{\left(\dfrac{1}{x} - \dfrac{1}{2}\right)}{x - 2}\right) = \lim\limits_{x \to 2}\left(\dfrac{\left(\dfrac{2-x}{2x}\right)}{x - 2}\right) = -\dfrac{1}{4}$

75.
$\lim\limits_{x \to 3}\left(\dfrac{\sqrt{3x+7} - 4}{x - 3}\right) = \dfrac{0}{0} = \lim\limits_{x \to 3}\left(\dfrac{\sqrt{3x+7} - 4}{x - 3}\right)\left(\dfrac{\sqrt{3x+7} + 4}{\sqrt{3x+7} + 4}\right) =$

$\lim\limits_{x \to 3}\left(\dfrac{1}{x-3}\right)\left(\dfrac{3x - 9}{\sqrt{3x+7} + 4}\right) = \lim\limits_{x \to 3}\left(\dfrac{1}{x-3}\right)\left(\dfrac{3(x-3)}{\sqrt{3x+7} + 4}\right) = \dfrac{3}{8}$

76. $\lim\limits_{x \to 4}\left(\dfrac{\sqrt{x+5} - 3}{\sqrt{x} + 3}\right) = \dfrac{0}{5} = 0$

77. $\lim\limits_{x \to -1}\left(\dfrac{x^2 + 2x + 1}{x^3 + 3x^2 + 3x + 1}\right) = \dfrac{0}{0} = \lim\limits_{x \to -1}\left(\dfrac{(x+1)^2}{(x+1)^3}\right) = \dfrac{1}{0} = D.E.(\pm\infty)$

78. $\lim\limits_{x \to 0}\left(\sin(x)\right) = 0$

79. $\lim\limits_{x \to 0}\left(\dfrac{1}{\cos(x)}\right) = 1$

80. $\lim\limits_{x \to 0}\left(\dfrac{2}{3 + e^{-\frac{1}{x}}}\right) = D.E.$ $\lim\limits_{x \to 0^+}\left(\dfrac{2}{3 + e^{-\frac{1}{x}}}\right) = \dfrac{2}{3}$ $\lim\limits_{x \to 0^-}\left(\dfrac{2}{3 + e^{-\frac{1}{x}}}\right) = 0$

81. $\lim\limits_{x \to 0}\left(\dfrac{1}{\sin(x)}\right) = D.E.(\pm\infty)$

• Check this limit on both "sides" of 0.

82. Use software or GDC to sketch a few of the functions and observe their behavior around the relevant point.

LATERAL LIMITS

83. $\lim\limits_{x\to 0}\left(\dfrac{1}{x}\right) = D.E$: Since this limit cannot be obtained we check the <u>lateral limits</u>:

$$\lim_{x\to 0^-}\left(\frac{1}{x}\right) = -\infty \qquad \lim_{x\to 0^+}\left(\frac{1}{x}\right) = \infty \text{, since different, limit does not exist.}$$

84. $\lim\limits_{x\to 0}\left(\dfrac{x}{|x|}\right) = \dfrac{0}{0}$ Since this limit cannot be obtained we check the <u>lateral limits</u>:

$$\lim_{x\to 0^-}\left(\frac{x}{-x}\right) = -1 \qquad \lim_{x\to 0^+}\left(\frac{x}{x}\right) = 1 \text{, since different, limit does not exist.}$$

Find the following limits, if possible:

85. $\lim\limits_{x\to 0}\left(\dfrac{x-2}{|x-2|}\right) = \dfrac{-2}{2} = -1$

86. $\lim\limits_{x\to -2}\left(\dfrac{3}{x+2}\right) = D.E. \qquad \lim\limits_{x\to -2^-}\left(\dfrac{3}{x+2}\right) = -\infty \qquad \lim\limits_{x\to -2^+}\left(\dfrac{1}{x+2}\right) = \infty$

87. $\lim\limits_{x\to -2}\left(\dfrac{3x+6}{x+2}\right) = \lim\limits_{x\to -2}\left(\dfrac{3(x+2)}{x+2}\right) = 3$

88. $\lim\limits_{x\to 2^+}\left(\dfrac{4-2x}{|4-2x|}\right) = \lim\limits_{x\to 2^+}\left(\dfrac{4-2x}{-(4-2x)}\right) = -1$

89. $\lim\limits_{x\to 1^-}\left(\dfrac{\sqrt{2}-\sqrt{2}x}{|\sqrt{2}-\sqrt{2}x|}\right) = \lim\limits_{x\to 1^-}\left(\dfrac{\sqrt{2}-\sqrt{2}x}{\sqrt{2}-\sqrt{2}x}\right) = 1$

90. $\lim\limits_{x\to 0}\left(\dfrac{1}{x} - \dfrac{1}{|x|}\right) = D.E. \qquad \lim\limits_{x\to 0^-}\left(\dfrac{1}{x} + \dfrac{1}{x}\right) = -\infty \qquad \lim\limits_{x\to 0^+}\left(\dfrac{1}{x} - \dfrac{1}{x}\right) = 0$

Lateral limits should be checked in case <u>the limit cannot be calculated and/or we suspect it does not exist.</u>

L´HOPITAL RULE $\lim\limits_{x\to a}\left(\dfrac{f(x)}{g(x)}\right) = \lim\limits_{x\to a}\left(\dfrac{f'(x)}{g'(x)}\right)$ applies **only** if $\left(\dfrac{0}{0}\right)$ or $\left(\dfrac{\pm\infty}{\pm\infty}\right)$

91. $\lim\limits_{\theta\to 0}\left(\dfrac{\sin\theta}{\theta}\right) = \dfrac{0}{0} = \lim\limits_{\theta\to 0}\left(\dfrac{\cos\theta}{1}\right) = 1$

92. $\lim\limits_{\theta\to 0}\left(\dfrac{1-\sin\theta}{\tan\theta}\right) = \dfrac{1}{0} = D.E.$

93.
$$\lim_{x\to 0}\left(\frac{e^x - e^{-x} - 2x}{x - \sin(x)}\right) = \frac{0}{0} = \lim_{x\to 0}\left(\frac{e^x + e^{-x} - 2}{1 - \cos(x)}\right) = \frac{0}{0} = \lim_{x\to 0}\left(\frac{e^x - e^{-x}}{\sin(x)}\right) =$$

$$= \frac{0}{0} = \lim_{x\to 0}\left(\frac{e^x + e^{-x}}{\cos(x)}\right) = 2$$

94. $\lim\limits_{\theta \to 0}\left(\dfrac{\csc\theta - \cot\theta}{\theta\csc\theta}\right) = \lim\limits_{\theta \to 0}\left(\dfrac{\dfrac{1-\cos\theta}{\sin\theta}}{\dfrac{\theta}{\sin\theta}}\right) = \lim\limits_{\theta \to 0}\left(\dfrac{1-\cos\theta}{\theta}\right) = \dfrac{0}{0} = \lim\limits_{\theta \to 0}\left(\dfrac{\sin\theta}{1}\right) = \dfrac{0}{1} = 0$

95. $\lim\limits_{x \to 0}\left(\dfrac{e^x - e^{-x} - 6x}{\sin(x)}\right) = \dfrac{0}{0} = \lim\limits_{x \to 0}\left(\dfrac{e^x + e^{-x} - 6}{\cos(x)}\right) = -4$

96. $\lim\limits_{\theta \to 0}\left(\dfrac{1 - \cos^2(\theta)}{\theta(1 + \cos(\theta))}\right) = \dfrac{0}{0} = \lim\limits_{\theta \to 0}\left(\dfrac{2\sin(\theta)\cos(\theta)}{1 + \cos(\theta) - \theta\sin(\theta)}\right) = \dfrac{0}{2} = 0$

97. $\lim\limits_{x \to \infty}\left(\dfrac{a}{x\sin\left(\dfrac{1}{x}\right)}\right) = \lim\limits_{x \to \infty}\left(\dfrac{ax^{-1}}{\sin\left(\dfrac{1}{x}\right)}\right) = \dfrac{0}{0} = \lim\limits_{x \to \infty}\left(\dfrac{-ax^{-2}}{-\cos\left(\dfrac{1}{x}\right)x^{-2}}\right) = a$

98. $\lim\limits_{x \to \infty}\left(\dfrac{\ln(2^x + 3^x)}{x}\right) = \dfrac{\infty}{\infty} = \lim\limits_{x \to \infty}\left(\dfrac{\left(\dfrac{2^x\ln(2) + 3^x\ln(3)}{2^x + 3^x}\right)}{1}\right) = \ln(3)$

99. $\lim\limits_{\theta \to 0}\left(\dfrac{\sec\theta}{\theta\csc\theta}\right) = \lim\limits_{\theta \to 0}\left(\dfrac{\sin(\theta)}{\theta\cos(\theta)}\right) = \dfrac{0}{0} = \lim\limits_{\theta \to 0}\left(\dfrac{\cos(\theta)}{\cos(\theta) - \theta\sin(\theta)}\right) = 1 =$

100. $\lim\limits_{t \to 0}\left(\dfrac{\sin 5t}{t}\right) = \dfrac{0}{0} = \lim\limits_{t \to 0}\left(\dfrac{5\cos 5t}{1}\right) = 5$

101. $\lim\limits_{\theta \to 0}\left(\dfrac{\sin(\cos\theta)}{\sec\theta}\right) = \sin(1)$

102. $\lim\limits_{\theta \to 0}\left(\dfrac{\sin^2\theta}{\theta}\right) = \dfrac{0}{0} = \lim\limits_{\theta \to 0}\left(\dfrac{2\sin(\theta)\cos(\theta)}{1}\right) = \dfrac{0}{1} = 0$

103. $\lim\limits_{x \to 0}\left(\dfrac{\cot 2x}{\csc x}\right) = \lim\limits_{x \to 0}\left(\dfrac{\sin(x)\cos(2x)}{\sin(2x)}\right) = \lim\limits_{x \to 0}\left(\dfrac{\sin(x)\cos(2x)}{2\sin(x)\cos(x)}\right) = \dfrac{1}{2}$

104. $\lim\limits_{\theta \to 0}\left(\dfrac{\sin(\theta)}{\theta + \tan(\theta)}\right) = \dfrac{0}{0} = \lim\limits_{\theta \to 0}\left(\dfrac{\cos(\theta)}{1 + \dfrac{1}{\cos^2(\theta)}}\right) = \dfrac{1}{2}$

105. $\lim\limits_{\theta \to 0}\left(\dfrac{\tan 2\theta}{\theta}\right) = \dfrac{0}{0} = \lim\limits_{\theta \to 0}\left(\dfrac{2}{\cos^2(2\theta)}\right) = 2$

106. $\lim\limits_{x \to 0}\left(\dfrac{x}{1 - \sqrt{x+1}}\right) = \dfrac{0}{0} = \lim\limits_{x \to 0}\dfrac{1}{\left(\dfrac{1}{2}(x+1)^{-\frac{1}{2}}\right)} = 2$ (possible without lhopital)

107. $\lim\limits_{x \to 0}\left(\dfrac{\sqrt{1-x}-\sqrt{1+x}}{x}\right) = \dfrac{0}{0} = \lim\limits_{x \to 0}\left(-\dfrac{1}{2}(1-x)^{-\frac{1}{2}} - \dfrac{1}{2}(1+x)^{-\frac{1}{2}}\right) = -1$ (possible without lhopital)

108. $\lim\limits_{x \to 1}\left(\dfrac{x^4-1}{x^2-1}\right) = \dfrac{0}{0} = \lim\limits_{x \to 1}\left(\dfrac{4x^3}{2x}\right) = 2$ (possible without lhopital)

109. $\lim\limits_{x \to 1}\left(\dfrac{x^5-1}{x^2-1}\right) = \dfrac{0}{0} = \lim\limits_{x \to 1}\left(\dfrac{5x^4}{2x}\right) = \dfrac{5}{2}$ (possible without lhopital)

110. $\lim\limits_{x \to 1}\left(\dfrac{2x^2-4x+2}{6x^2-6}\right) = \dfrac{0}{0} = \lim\limits_{x \to 1}\left(\dfrac{4x-4}{12x}\right) = \dfrac{0}{12} = 0$ (possible without lhopital)

111. $\lim\limits_{x \to \infty}\left(\dfrac{x^3-1}{x^2-1}\right) = \infty$

112. $\lim\limits_{x \to 0}\left(\dfrac{\sin(\sin(x))}{\sin(x^2)}\right) = \dfrac{0}{0} = \lim\limits_{x \to 0}\left(\dfrac{\cos(\sin(x))\cos(x)}{2x\cos(x^2)}\right) = \dfrac{1}{0} = D.E.$

113. $\lim\limits_{x \to 1}\left(\dfrac{\ln(x)}{x-1}\right) = \dfrac{0}{0} = \lim\limits_{x \to 1}\left(\dfrac{x^{-1}}{1}\right) = 1$

114. $\lim\limits_{x \to 7}\left(\dfrac{x^2-8x+7}{x-7}\right) = \dfrac{0}{0} = \lim\limits_{x \to 7}\left(\dfrac{2x-8}{1}\right) = 6$ (possible without lhopital)

115. $\lim\limits_{x \to 1}\left(\dfrac{\cos^2\left(\dfrac{\pi x}{2}\right)}{(x-1)^2}\right) = \dfrac{0}{0} = \lim\limits_{x \to 1}\left(\dfrac{-\pi\sin\left(\dfrac{\pi x}{2}\right)\cos\left(\dfrac{\pi x}{2}\right)}{2(x-1)}\right) = \dfrac{0}{0} =$

$\lim\limits_{x \to 1}\dfrac{\left(\dfrac{-\pi^2}{2}\cos\left(\dfrac{\pi x}{2}\right)\cos\left(\dfrac{\pi x}{2}\right) + \dfrac{\pi^2}{2}\sin\left(\dfrac{\pi x}{2}\right)\sin\left(\dfrac{\pi x}{2}\right)\right)}{2} = \dfrac{\pi^2}{4}$

116. $\lim\limits_{x \to 0}\left(\dfrac{\sin(x)-\ln(x+1)}{x^2 e^x}\right) = \dfrac{0}{0} = \lim\limits_{x \to 0}\left(\dfrac{\cos(x)-(x+1)^{-1}}{(2x+x^2)e^x}\right) = \dfrac{0}{0} = \lim\limits_{x \to 0}\left(\dfrac{-\sin(x)+(x+1)^{-2}}{(2+4x+x^2)e^x}\right) = \dfrac{1}{2}$

117. $\lim\limits_{x \to 0}\left(\dfrac{e^x-\ln(x+e)}{\sin(2x)}\right) = \dfrac{0}{0} = \lim\limits_{x \to 0}\left(\dfrac{e^x-(x+e)^{-1}}{2\cos(2x)}\right) = \dfrac{1-e^{-1}}{2}$

118. $\lim\limits_{x \to 0}\left(\dfrac{e^{4x}-2e^{2x}+1}{(\sin(3x))^2}\right) = \dfrac{0}{0} = \lim\limits_{x \to 0}\left(\dfrac{4e^{4x}-4e^{2x}}{6\sin(3x)\cos(3x)}\right) = \dfrac{0}{0} =$

$\lim\limits_{x \to 0}\left(\dfrac{16e^{4x}-8e^{2x}}{18\cos(3x)\cos(3x)-18\sin(3x)\sin(3x)}\right) = \dfrac{8}{18}$

1.2. – SEQUENCES AND SERIES

1. The following numbers 3, 7, 11, 15, …form an <u>arithmetic sequence</u>
2. A **sequence** whose terms tend to <u>0</u> is called convergent. Otherwise the sequence is called <u>divergent</u>
3. The corresponding **series** is 3 + 7 <u>+ 11 + 15 + …</u>
4. Given the following **sequences**, determine if the sequence is convergent and write the corresponding sum.
   a. 1, 2, 3, 4… Convergent / **Divergent**, Corresponding sum: 1 + 2 + 3 + …
   b. 5, 10, 15, 20, 25, 30 Convergent / **Divergent**, Corresponding sum: 5 + 10 + ..
   c. 5, 10, 20, 40 … Convergent / **Divergent**, Corresponding sum: 5 + 10 + 20 …
   d. 200, –100, 50, –25, … **Convergent** / Divergent, Corresponding sum: 200 – 100 + 50 – 25 ….
   e. $\dfrac{1}{2}, \dfrac{2}{4}, \dfrac{3}{8}, \dfrac{4}{16}$… **Convergent** / Divergent, Corresponding sum: $\dfrac{1}{2}+\dfrac{2}{4}+\dfrac{3}{8}+\dfrac{4}{16}$…
   f. 12, 10, 8, 6… –100. Convergent / **Divergent**, Corresponding sum: 12 + 10…
   g. 10, 1, 0.1, 0.01, 0.001, 0.0001 **Convergent** / Divergent, Corresponding sum: 10 + 1 + 0.1 + 0.01 + …
   h. $\dfrac{1}{1}, \dfrac{1}{2}, \dfrac{1}{3}, \dfrac{1}{4}, …, \dfrac{1}{122}$ **Convergent** / Divergent, Corresponding sum: $\dfrac{1}{1}+\dfrac{1}{2}+\dfrac{1}{3}$…
   i. $\dfrac{7}{5}, -\dfrac{7}{10}, \dfrac{7}{20}, -\dfrac{7}{40}, …, \dfrac{7}{1280}$ **Convergent** / Divergent, Corresponding sum:
   $\dfrac{7}{5} - \dfrac{7}{10} + \dfrac{7}{20} - \dfrac{7}{40} + …$
   j. 6, 10, 14, …,118 Convergent / **Divergent**, Corresponding sum: 6 + 10 + 14…
5. **Series** are often written using <u>Sigma notation</u>

   For example the series 3 + 7 + 11 + 15 + … can be written: $\displaystyle\sum_{k=1}^{\infty} 4k - 1$

6. Write the following **series** using sigma notation, if the series is arithmetic or geometric, find the sum:

   k. $1 + 2 + 3 + 4…. = \displaystyle\sum_{k=1}^{\infty} k = S_n = \dfrac{n}{2}(2+(n-1))$

   l. $4 + 3 + 2 + 1 + … = \displaystyle\sum_{k=1}^{\infty} 5 - k = S_n = \dfrac{n}{2}(8-(n-1))$

   m. $5 + 10 + 15 + 20 + 25 + 30 = \displaystyle\sum_{k=1}^{\infty} 5 + 5k = S_n = \dfrac{n}{2}(10+5(n-1))$

   n. $5 + 10 + 20 + 40 + … = \displaystyle\sum_{k=1}^{\infty} 5 \cdot 2^{k-1} = S_n = \dfrac{5(2^n - 1)}{2 - 1}$

   o. $200 - 100 + 50 - 25 + … = \displaystyle\sum_{k=1}^{\infty} 200 \cdot \left(-\dfrac{1}{2}\right)^{k-1} = S_\infty = \dfrac{200}{1-\left(-\dfrac{1}{2}\right)} = \dfrac{400}{3}$

   p. $\dfrac{1}{2}+\dfrac{2}{4}+\dfrac{3}{8}+\dfrac{4}{16}+… = \displaystyle\sum_{k=1}^{\infty} \dfrac{k}{2 \cdot 2^{k-1}}$

   q. $12 + 10 + 8 + … -100 = \displaystyle\sum_{k=1}^{57} 14 - 2k = S_{57} = \dfrac{57}{2}(24 - 2(57-1)) = -2508$

r. $10 + 1 + 0.1 + 0.01 + 0.001 + 0.0001 = \sum_{k=1}^{\infty} 10 \cdot \left(\frac{1}{10}\right)^{k-1} = S_{\infty} = \frac{10}{1 - \left(\frac{1}{10}\right)} = \frac{100}{9}$

s. $\frac{1}{1} + \frac{1}{2} + \frac{1}{3} + \frac{1}{4} + \ldots + \frac{1}{122} = \sum_{k=1}^{122} \left(\frac{1}{k}\right)$

t. $\frac{7}{5} - \frac{7}{10} + \frac{7}{20} - \frac{7}{40} + \ldots \frac{7}{1280} = \sum_{k=1}^{9} \frac{7}{5} \cdot \left(-\frac{1}{2}\right)^{k-1} = S_9 = \frac{\frac{7}{5}\left(\left(-\frac{1}{2}\right)^8 - 1\right)}{\left(-\frac{1}{2}\right) - 1} = \frac{119}{128}$

u. $6 + 10 + 14 + \ldots + 118 = \sum_{k=1}^{29} 2 + 4k = S_{29} = \frac{29}{2}(12 + 4(29-1)) = 1798$

v. $\frac{1}{e} - \frac{1}{e^2} + \frac{1}{e^3} - \frac{1}{e^4} + \ldots = \sum_{k=1}^{\infty} \frac{1}{e} \cdot \left(-\frac{1}{e}\right)^{k-1} = S_{\infty} = \frac{e^{-1}}{1 - \left(-\frac{1}{e}\right)} = \frac{1}{e+1}$

7. Write each series using sigma notation:

   a. $1 + 8 + 27 + 81 + \ldots = \sum_{i=1}^{i=\infty} 1 \cdot 3^{i-1}$

   b. $15 + 19 + 23 + 27 + 31 + 35 + 39 + 43 = \sum_{i=1}^{i=8} 11 + 4i$

   c. $1 + \frac{1}{9} + \frac{1}{81} + \ldots = \sum_{i=1}^{i=\infty} 1 \cdot \left(\frac{1}{9}\right)^{i-1}$

8. $13 + 16 + 19 + 22 + \ldots$ for 28 terms. $\sum_{i=1}^{i=28} 10 + 3i = \frac{28}{2}(26 + 3(28-1)) = 1498$

9. $-30 + 60 - 120 + 240 - 480 + \ldots$ for 35 terms. $\sum_{i=1}^{i=35} -30 \cdot (-2)^{i-1} = \frac{-30((-2)^{35} - 1)}{-2 - 1}$

10. $18.13 + 18.11 + 18.09 + 18.07 + \ldots$ for 100 terms.

$$\sum_{i=1}^{i=100} 18.15 - 0.02i = \frac{100}{2}(36.3 - 0.02(100-1)) = 1716$$

11. The following **sequence** $1, \frac{1}{2}, \frac{1}{3}, \frac{1}{4}, \ldots$ is <u>convergent</u> (its terms tend to 0). Its

    corresponding series $\sum_{n=1}^{\infty} \frac{1}{n} = 1 + \frac{1}{2} + \frac{1}{3} + \frac{1}{4} + \ldots$ is called the <u>harmonic</u>

    series. It is **divergent**, which means the sum **does not add up to** a <u>number</u>

12. So as can be seen in the previous example even if the general term of a sequence tends to <u>0</u> it does not mean the corresponding series will add up to a <u>number</u> (that is, will be convergent).

13. The following **sequence** $1, \frac{1}{4}, \frac{1}{9}, \frac{1}{16}, \ldots$ is <u>convergent</u> (its terms tend to 0). The

    corresponding series $\sum_{n=1}^{\infty} \frac{1}{n^2} = 1 + \frac{1}{4} + \frac{1}{9} + \frac{1}{16} + \ldots$, (calculated by Leonard Euler) is **convergent** , which means the sum **adds up to** a number. In fact this is a famous sum that as Euler proved adds up to $\dfrac{\pi^2}{6}$

14. A series is convergent if <u>the sum of all the terms adds up to a number</u>
15. A series is divergent if <u>the sum of all the terms does not add up to a number</u>
16. If the general term of a **sequence** tends to 0 the **corresponding series** may be <u>convergent</u> or <u>divergent</u>
17. If the general term of a **sequence** does not tend to 0 the **corresponding series** will be <u>divergent</u>
18. Determine if the general term tends to 0 and in consequence write down which of the following series diverge.

   a. $\displaystyle\sum_{n=1}^{\infty}\frac{2n}{3n+1}$ $Divergent$ $Lim_{n\to\infty}\left(\dfrac{2n}{3n+1}\right)=\dfrac{2}{3}$

   b. $\displaystyle\sum_{n=1}^{\infty}\frac{n}{3n^2+n+2}$ $Divergent$ $\displaystyle\sum_{n=1}^{\infty}\frac{n}{3n^2+n+2}>\sum_{n=1}^{\infty}\frac{n}{1000n^2}$ $P-series$

   c. $\displaystyle\sum_{n=2}^{\infty}1+\frac{1}{\ln(n)}$ $Divergent$ $Lim_{n\to\infty}\left(1+\dfrac{1}{\ln(n)}\right)=1$

   d. $\displaystyle\sum_{n=1}^{\infty}5\frac{3^{n+3}}{4^{n-1}}=\sum_{n=1}^{\infty}20\cdot27\left(\frac{3}{4}\right)^{n}=540\dfrac{\left(\frac{3}{4}\right)}{1-\left(\frac{3}{4}\right)}=1620$ $Convergent$ $Geometric$

   e. $\displaystyle\sum_{n=1}^{\infty}n+1$ $Divergent$ $Lim_{n\to\infty}(n+1)=\infty$

   f. $\displaystyle\sum_{n=1}^{\infty}\frac{5\sqrt{n}+1}{\sqrt{n}}$ $Divergent$ $Lim_{n\to\infty}\left(\dfrac{5\sqrt{n}+1}{\sqrt{n}}\right)=5$

   g. $\displaystyle\sum_{n=1}^{\infty}\frac{5n}{n^3\sqrt{n}}=\sum_{n=1}^{\infty}\frac{5}{n^{\frac{7}{6}}}$ $Convergent$ $P-series$

   h. $\displaystyle\sum_{n=1}^{\infty}\frac{6^{n+3}+2^n+1}{5^{n-1}}=\sum_{n=1}^{\infty}1080\left(\frac{6}{5}\right)^{n}+5\left(\frac{2}{5}\right)^{n}+5\left(\frac{1}{5}\right)^{n}$ $Divergent$ $\dfrac{6}{5}>1$ $(Geometric)$

   i. $\displaystyle\sum_{n=1}^{\infty}\frac{\sin(\pi n)}{n^2}$ $convergent$ $\displaystyle\sum_{n=1}^{\infty}\frac{\sin(\pi n)}{n^2}<\sum_{n=1}^{\infty}\frac{1}{n^2}$ $P-series$

   j. $\displaystyle\sum_{n=1}^{\infty}\frac{\cos(\pi n)}{n^2}$ $convergent$ $\displaystyle\sum_{n=1}^{\infty}\frac{\cos(\pi n)}{n^2}<\sum_{n=1}^{\infty}\frac{1}{n^2}$ $P-series$

   k. $\displaystyle\sum_{n-1}^{\infty}\frac{\cos(\pi n)}{2^n}$ $convergent$ $\displaystyle\sum_{n=5}^{\infty}\frac{\cos(\pi n)}{2^n}<\sum_{n=5}^{\infty}\frac{1}{n^2}$

   l. $\displaystyle\sum_{n=1}^{\infty}\frac{8}{9^n}=\sum_{n=1}^{\infty}8\left(\frac{1}{9}\right)^{n}=8\dfrac{\left(\frac{1}{9}\right)}{\left(1-\frac{1}{9}\right)}=1$

   m. $\displaystyle\sum_{n=1}^{\infty}\frac{\cos\left(\frac{1}{n}\right)}{n}$ $Divergent$ Equivalent to harmonic series

1.3. – THE P-SERIES

1. The **series** $\displaystyle\sum_{n=1}^{\infty}\frac{1}{n^p}=1+\frac{1}{2^p}+\frac{1}{3^p}+\frac{1}{4^p}+...$ is called the P – Series

2. This series was studied a lot and the following conclusions deduced:
    If **p ≤ 1** it is **divergent**, which means the sum **does not add up to** a number
    If **p ≥ 1** it is **convergent**, which means the sum **adds up to** a number

3. If p = 1 it is called the harmonic series.

Determine if the following series converge or diverge:

4. $\displaystyle\sum_{n=1}^{n=\infty} n$ $Divergent\left(\lim_{n\to\infty}(n)\neq 0\right)$

5. $\displaystyle\sum_{n=1}^{n=\infty}\frac{1}{\sqrt{n}}$ $Divergent\ (P-series)$

6. $\displaystyle\sum_{n=1}^{n=\infty}\frac{1}{\sqrt[3]{n}}$ $Divergent\ (P-series)$

7. $\displaystyle\sum_{n=1}^{n=\infty}\frac{1}{n^3}$ $Convergent\ (P-series)$

8. $\displaystyle\sum_{n=1}^{n=\infty}\frac{1}{n^{0.999}}$ $Divergent\ (P-series)$

9. $\displaystyle\sum_{n=1}^{n=\infty}\frac{1}{n\sqrt{n}}$ $Convergent\ (P-series)$

10. $\displaystyle\sum_{n=1}^{n=\infty}\frac{1}{n^{\frac{20}{31}}}$ $Divergent\ (P-series)$

11. $\displaystyle\sum_{n=1}^{n=\infty}\frac{1}{\sqrt[17]{n^2}}$ $Divergent\ (P-series)$

12. $\displaystyle\sum_{n=1}^{n=\infty}\frac{1}{\sqrt[7]{n^2}\,n^{0.80}}$ $Convergent$
    $(P-series)$

13. $\displaystyle\sum_{n=1}^{n=\infty}\frac{1}{n}$ $Divergent\ (P-series)$

14. $\displaystyle\sum_{n=1}^{n=\infty}\left(\frac{1}{2}\right)^n$ $Convergent(Geometric)$

15. $\displaystyle\sum_{n=1}^{n=\infty} e^n$ $Divergent\left(\lim_{n\to\infty}(n)\neq 0\right)$

16. $\displaystyle\sum_{n=1}^{n=\infty} \sin(n)$ $Divergent\left(\lim_{n\to\infty}(n)\neq 0\right)$

17. $\displaystyle\sum_{n=1}^{n=\infty}\frac{1}{n^2}$ $Convergent\ (P-series)$

18. $\displaystyle\sum_{n=1}^{n=\infty} 5\left(\frac{2}{3}\right)^n$ $Convergent(Geometric)$

19. $\displaystyle\sum_{n=1}^{n=\infty} 2n+1$ $Divergent\left(\lim_{n\to\infty}(n)\neq 0\right)$

20. $\displaystyle\sum_{n=1}^{n=\infty} \sqrt{n}$ $Divergent\left(\lim_{n\to\infty}(n)\neq 0\right)$

21. $\displaystyle\sum_{n=1}^{n=\infty} \ln(n)$ $Divergent\left(\lim_{n\to\infty}(n)\neq 0\right)$

22. $\displaystyle\sum_{n=1}^{n=\infty} \sin(\frac{1}{n})$
    $Convergent\ (\sin(x)\approx x, x\ll 1)$

23. $\displaystyle\sum_{n=1}^{n=\infty} 2\left(\frac{7}{6}\right)^n$ $Divergent(Geometric)$

24. $\displaystyle\sum_{n=1}^{n=\infty} \ln(\frac{1}{n})$ $Divergent\left(\lim_{n\to\infty}(n)\neq 0\right)$

25. $\displaystyle\sum_{n=1}^{n=\infty} 1200\left(-\frac{1}{6}\right)^n$
    $Convergent(Geometric)$

26. $\displaystyle\sum_{n=1}^{n=\infty} e^{\frac{1}{n}}$ $Divergent\left(\lim_{n\to\infty}(n)\neq 0\right)$

27. $\displaystyle\sum_{n=1}^{n=\infty} 2^n$ $Divergent\left(\lim_{n\to\infty}(n)\neq 0\right)$

28. $\displaystyle\sum_{n=1}^{n=\infty} \left(-\frac{11}{8}\right)^n$ $Divergent(Geometric)$

29. $\displaystyle\sum_{n=1}^{\infty} \frac{2n}{3n^2}$ $Divergent\ (P-series)$

30. $\displaystyle\sum_{n=1}^{\infty} \frac{n^2}{5n^2+2}$ $Divergent\left(\lim_{n\to\infty}(n)\neq 0\right)$

31. $\displaystyle\sum_{n=2}^{\infty} \frac{\sqrt{n}}{\sqrt[3]{n}}$ $Divergent\left(\lim_{n\to\infty}(n)\neq 0\right)$

32. $\displaystyle\sum_{n=1}^{n=\infty} 2^{-n}$ $Convergent(Geometric)$

33. $\displaystyle\sum_{n=1}^{\infty}\frac{n^2+n}{3n^3}=\sum_{n=1}^{\infty}\frac{1}{3n}+\frac{1}{3n^2}$

$Divergent(P-series)$

34. $\displaystyle\sum_{n=1}^{\infty}\frac{n\sqrt{n^3}}{2\sqrt{n}\cdot n^2}=\sum_{n=1}^{\infty}\frac{1}{2\cdot n^{\frac{7}{6}}}$

$Convergent\,(P-series)$

35. $\displaystyle\sum_{n=1}^{\infty}\frac{3n^2+2n+1}{5n^2+3n+4}$

$Divergent\left(\lim_{n\to\infty}(n)\neq 0\right)$

36. $\displaystyle\sum_{n=1}^{\infty}\frac{\sin(n\pi)+n^2}{-n^4}=-\sum_{n=1}^{\infty}\frac{\sin(n\pi)}{n^4}+\frac{1}{n^2}$

$\displaystyle\sum_{n=1}^{\infty}\frac{\sin(n\pi)}{n^4}+\frac{1}{n^2}<\sum_{n=1}^{\infty}\frac{1}{n^4}+\frac{1}{n^2}$

$Convergent\,(P-series)$

$\displaystyle\sum_{n=1}^{\infty}\frac{\cos(n\pi)-n^2}{n^3}=\sum_{n=1}^{\infty}\frac{\cos(n\pi)}{n^3}-\frac{1}{n}\quad Divergent$

37. $\displaystyle\sum_{n=1}^{\infty}\frac{\cos(n\pi)}{n^3}\quad Convergent$

$-\displaystyle\sum_{n=1}^{\infty}\frac{1}{n}\quad Divergent$

38. $\displaystyle\sum_{n=1}^{\infty}\frac{8\sqrt[5]{n}\cdot n^2}{5n\sqrt[3]{n}}=\sum_{n=1}^{\infty}\frac{8}{5}n^{\frac{13}{15}}$

$Divergent\,(P-series)$

1.4. – CONVERGENCE TESTS

1. In order to check if a certain series converges or diverges we will use one of the following tests.
2. Use the Comparison Test to determine, if possible, convergence/divergence of the series, comment if other tests are more suitable.

a. $\displaystyle\sum_{n=1}^{n=\infty}\frac{2}{n+1} < \sum_{n=1}^{n=\infty}\frac{2}{n}$ Divergent

f. $\displaystyle\sum_{n=1}^{n=\infty}\frac{n+2}{n+1}$ Divergent $\left(\lim_{x\to\infty}(n)\neq 0\right)$

b. $\displaystyle\sum_{n=2}^{n=\infty}\frac{1}{n-1} \leq \sum_{n=1}^{n=\infty}\frac{1}{n}$ Divergent

g. $\displaystyle\sum_{n=1}^{n=\infty}\frac{5}{3^{n-1}+n} < \sum_{n=1}^{n=\infty}\frac{5}{3^{n-1}}$ Convergent

c. $\displaystyle\sum_{n=1}^{n=\infty}\frac{1}{n\cdot 2^n} < \sum_{n=1}^{n=\infty}\frac{1}{2^n}$ Convergent

h. $\displaystyle\sum_{n=2}^{n=\infty}\frac{1}{\ln(n)(0.5)^{n-1}e^n} = \sum_{n=2}^{n=\infty}\frac{2}{\ln(n)}\left(\frac{2}{e}\right)^n$

d. $\displaystyle\sum_{n=1}^{n=\infty}\frac{2^n}{\ln(2)}$ Divergent $\left(\lim_{x\to\infty}(a_n)\neq 0\right)$

$\displaystyle\sum_{n=8}^{n=\infty}\frac{2}{\ln(n)}\left(\frac{2}{e}\right)^n < \sum_{n=8}^{n=\infty}\left(\frac{2}{e}\right)^n$

e. $\displaystyle\sum_{n=1}^{n=\infty}\frac{1}{\ln(n)\cdot 3^n} < \sum_{n=1}^{n=\infty}\frac{1}{3^n}$ Convergent

3. Use the Ratio Test to determine, if possible, convergence/divergence of the series, comment if other tests are more suitable.

a. $\displaystyle\sum_{n=1}^{n=\infty}\frac{1}{n!}$ Convergent $\displaystyle\lim_{n\to\infty}\left|\frac{a_{n+1}}{a_n}\right| = \lim_{n\to\infty}\left|\frac{n!}{(n+1)!}\right| = \lim_{n\to\infty}\left|\frac{1}{(n+1)}\right| = 0$

b. $\displaystyle\sum_{n=1}^{n=\infty}\frac{2^n}{n}$ Divergent $\displaystyle\lim_{n\to\infty}\left|\frac{a_{n+1}}{a_n}\right| = \lim_{n\to\infty}\left|\frac{2^{n+1}n}{2^n(n+1)}\right| = \lim_{n\to\infty}\left|\frac{2n}{n+1}\right| = 2$

c. $\displaystyle\sum_{n=2}^{n=\infty}\frac{1}{\ln(n)} > \sum_{n=2}^{n=\infty}\frac{1}{n}$ Divergent $\displaystyle\lim_{n\to\infty}\left|\frac{a_{n+1}}{a_n}\right| = \lim_{n\to\infty}\left|\frac{Ln(n)}{Ln(n+1)}\right| = 1(Test\ inconclusive)$

d. $\displaystyle\sum_{n=1}^{n=\infty}\frac{n}{3^{n+1}}(-1)^n$ Convergent $\displaystyle\lim_{n\to\infty}\left|\frac{a_{n+1}}{a_n}\right| = \lim_{n\to\infty}\left|\frac{3^{n+1}(n+1)(-1)^{n+1}}{3^{n+2}n(-1)^n}\right| = \lim_{n\to\infty}\left|\frac{(n+1)(-1)}{3n}\right| = \frac{1}{3}$

e. $\displaystyle\sum_{n=1}^{n=\infty}\frac{1}{\sqrt{n}}$ Divergent$(P-series)$ $\displaystyle\lim_{n\to\infty}\left|\frac{a_{n+1}}{a_n}\right| = \lim_{n\to\infty}\left|\frac{\sqrt{n}}{\sqrt{n+1}}\right| = 1(Test\ inconclusive)$

f. $\displaystyle\sum_{n=1}^{n=\infty}n!$ Divergent $\left(\lim_{n\to\infty}(a_n)\neq 0\right)$

g. $\displaystyle\sum_{n=1}^{n=\infty}\frac{1}{n\cdot 3^{n+1}}$ Convergent $\displaystyle\lim_{n\to\infty}\left|\frac{a_{n+1}}{a_n}\right| = \lim_{n\to\infty}\left|\frac{3^{n+1}n}{3^{n+2}(n+1)}\right| = \lim_{n\to\infty}\left|\frac{n}{3(n+1)}\right| = \frac{1}{3}$

h. $\displaystyle\sum_{n=1}^{n=\infty}\frac{n!}{5^n}$ Divergent $\displaystyle\lim_{n\to\infty}\left|\frac{a_{n+1}}{a_n}\right| = \lim_{n\to\infty}\left|\frac{5^n(n+1)!}{5^{n+1}n!}\right| = \lim_{n\to\infty}\left|\frac{(n+1)}{5}\right| = \infty$

i. $\displaystyle\sum_{n=1}^{n=\infty}\frac{1}{2^{n+1}\sqrt{n}}$ Convergent $\displaystyle\lim_{n\to\infty}\left|\frac{a_{n+1}}{a_n}\right| = \lim_{n\to\infty}\left|\frac{2^{n+1}\sqrt{n}}{2^{n+2}\sqrt{n+1}}\right| = \frac{1}{2}$

j. $\displaystyle\sum_{n=1}^{n=\infty} \frac{(-1)^n}{3^n \sqrt[3]{n}}$ *Convergent* $\displaystyle\lim_{n\to\infty}\left|\frac{a_{n+1}}{a_n}\right| = \lim_{n\to\infty}\left|\frac{3^n n^{\frac{1}{3}}(-1)^{n+1}}{3^{n+1}(n+1)^{\frac{1}{3}}(-1)^n}\right| = \frac{1}{3}$

k. $\displaystyle\sum_{n=1}^{n=\infty} \frac{n!}{n^n}$ *Convergent* $\displaystyle\lim_{n\to\infty}\left|\frac{a_{n+1}}{a_n}\right| = \lim_{n\to\infty}\left|\frac{n^n(n+1)!}{(n+1)^{n+1}n!}\right| = \lim_{n\to\infty}\left|\frac{n^n}{(n+1)^n}\right| = \lim_{n\to\infty}\left|\left(\frac{n}{n+1}\right)^n\right| = \frac{1}{e}$

l. $\displaystyle\sum_{n=1}^{n=\infty} \frac{n}{\ln(n)2^n}$ *Convergent* $\displaystyle\lim_{n\to\infty}\left|\frac{a_{n+1}}{a_n}\right| = \lim_{n\to\infty}\left|\frac{2^n \ln(n)\cdot(n+1)}{2^{n+1}\ln(n+1)\cdot n}\right| = \frac{1}{2}$

$\displaystyle\sum_{n=1}^{n=\infty} \frac{\ln(n)}{2^{\sqrt{n}}}$ *Convergent* $\displaystyle\sum_{n=3}^{n=\infty} \frac{\ln(n)}{2^{\sqrt{n}}} < \sum_{n=3}^{n=\infty} \frac{1}{\sqrt{n}\,2^{\sqrt{n}}}$

m. $\displaystyle\lim_{n\to\infty}\left|\frac{a_{n+1}}{a_n}\right| = \lim_{n\to\infty}\left|\frac{2^{\sqrt{n}}\ln(n+1)}{2^{\sqrt{n+1}}\ln(n)}\right| = 1$ *(Test inconclusive)*

Using Integral Test $\displaystyle Lim_{n\to\infty}\left(\int_1^n \frac{1}{\sqrt{t}\,2^{\sqrt{t}}}\,dt\right) = \frac{1}{\ln(2)}$

4. Use the Limit Comparison Test to determine, if possible, convergence/divergence of the series, comment if other tests are more suitable.

a. $\displaystyle\sum_{n=1}^{n=\infty} \frac{1}{n+1}$ $\displaystyle\lim_{n\to\infty}\left|\frac{\frac{1}{n+1}}{\frac{1}{n}}\right| = 1$ *Divergent (same behaviour)*

b. $\displaystyle\sum_{n=1}^{n=\infty} \frac{\sqrt{n}}{3n^2+3}$ $\displaystyle\lim_{n\to\infty}\left|\frac{\frac{\sqrt{n}}{3n^2+3}}{\frac{1}{n^{\frac{3}{2}}}}\right| = \frac{1}{3}$ *Convergent (same behaviour)*

c. $\displaystyle\sum_{n=1}^{n=\infty} \frac{n^2+4n}{2n^4+3n+1}$ $\displaystyle\lim_{n\to\infty}\left|\frac{\frac{n^2+4n}{2n^4+3n+1}}{\frac{1}{n^2}}\right| = \frac{1}{2}$ *Convergent (same behaviour)*

d. $\displaystyle\sum_{n=1}^{n=\infty} \frac{1}{3n+2^n}$ $\displaystyle\lim_{n\to\infty}\left|\frac{\frac{1}{3n+2^n}}{\frac{1}{2^n}}\right| = 1$ *Convergent (same behaviour)*

e. $\displaystyle\sum_{n=1}^{n=\infty} \frac{\cos(n\pi)}{3n+\sin(n)} = \sum_{n=1}^{n=\infty} \frac{(-1)^n}{3n+\sin(n)}$ *Convergent* (Alternating and general term tends to 0)

f. $\displaystyle\sum_{n=1}^{n=\infty} \frac{\sqrt{n}}{5+n+\ln(n)}$ $\displaystyle\lim_{n\to\infty}\left|\frac{\frac{\sqrt{n}}{5+n+\ln(n)}}{\frac{1}{\sqrt{n}}}\right| = 1$ *Divergent (same behaviour)*

106

g. $\displaystyle\sum_{n=1}^{n=\infty} \frac{3^n}{2^n + n + \ln(n)}$ $Divergent$ $\left(\lim_{n\to\infty}(\frac{3^n}{2^n + n + \ln(n)}) = \frac{3}{2} \right)$

5. Use the Integral Test to determine, if possible, convergence/divergence of the series, comment if other tests are more suitable. (This part can be done only after integration was taught)

a. $\displaystyle\sum_{n=1}^{n=\infty} \frac{1}{n^3}$ $Convergent$ $Lim_{n\to\infty}\int_1^n \frac{1}{t^3}dt = Lim_{n\to\infty}\left[\frac{t^{-2}}{-2}\right]_1^n = \frac{1}{2}$

b. $\displaystyle\sum_{n=1}^{n=\infty} \frac{1}{n^{0.9}}$ $Divergent(P-series)$

c. $\displaystyle\sum_{n=2}^{n=\infty} \frac{1}{n\ln(n)}$ $Divergent$ $Lim_{n\to\infty}\int_2^n \frac{1}{t\ln(t)}dt = Lim_{n\to\infty}\left[\ln(\ln(t))\right]_2^n = \infty$

d. $\displaystyle\sum_{n=1}^{n=\infty} 2^{-n}$ $Convergent$ $Lim_{n\to\infty}\int_1^n 2^{-t}dt = Lim_{n\to\infty}\left[\frac{-2^{-t}}{\ln(2)}\right]_1^n = \frac{1}{2\ln(2)}$

e. $\displaystyle\sum_{n=1}^{n=\infty} \frac{\sin(n^{-1})}{n^2}$ $Convergent$ $Lim_{n\to\infty}\int_1^n \frac{\sin(t^{-1})}{t^2}dt = Lim_{n\to\infty}\left[\cos(t^{-1})\right]_1^n = 1 - \cos(1)$

f. $\displaystyle\sum_{n=1}^{n=\infty} \frac{1}{\sqrt[7]{n^2}n^{0.80}} = \sum_{n=1}^{n=\infty} \frac{1}{n^{\frac{38}{35}}}$ $Convergent$ $Lim_{n\to\infty}\int_1^n \frac{1}{t^{\frac{38}{35}}}dt = Lim_{n\to\infty}\left[-\frac{35}{3}t^{-\frac{3}{35}}\right]_1^n = \frac{35}{3}$

g. $\displaystyle\sum_{n=1}^{n=\infty} \frac{1}{2n-5}$ $Divergent$ $Lim_{n\to\infty}\int_3^n \frac{1}{2t-5}dt = Lim_{n\to\infty}\left[\frac{\ln(2t-5)}{2}\right]_1^n = \infty$

h. $\displaystyle\sum_{n=1}^{n=\infty} \left(\frac{1}{2}\right)^n$ $Convergent$ $Lim_{n\to\infty}\int_1^n 2^{-t}dt = Lim_{n\to\infty}\left[\frac{-2^{-t}}{\ln(2)}\right]_1^n = \frac{1}{2\ln(2)}$

i. $\displaystyle\sum_{n=1}^{n=\infty} e^{-n}\ln(e^{-n}+1)$ $Convergent$ $Lim_{n\to\infty}\int_1^n e^{-t}\ln(e^{-t}+1)dt = Lim_{n\to\infty}\left[-\ln(e^{-t}+1)\right]_1^n =$

$e^{-3}\ln(e^{-3}+1)+\ln(e^{-3}+1)-e^{-3}$

j. $\displaystyle\sum_{n=1}^{n=\infty} 2^{-n}\sin(2^{-n})$ $Convergent$ $Lim_{n\to\infty}\int_1^n 2^{-t}\sin(2^{-t})dt = Lim_{n\to\infty}\left[\frac{\cos(2^{-t})}{\ln(2)}\right]_1^n = \frac{1-\cos(\frac{1}{2})}{\ln(2)}$

k. $\displaystyle\sum_{n=1}^{n=\infty} \frac{1}{n^2+1}$ $Convergent$ $Lim_{n\to\infty}\int_1^n \frac{1}{t^2+1}dt = Lim_{n\to\infty}\left[\arctan(t)\right]_1^n = \frac{\pi}{4}$

l. $\displaystyle\sum_{n=1}^{n=\infty} \frac{n}{\sqrt{n^2-5}}$ $Divergent$ $Lim_{n\to\infty}\int_3^n \frac{t}{\sqrt{t^2-5}}dt = Lim_{n\to\infty}\left[\sqrt{t^2-5}\right]_3^n = \infty$

m. $\displaystyle\sum_{n=1}^{n=\infty} \frac{Ln(2+\frac{1}{n})}{n^2} < \sum_{n=1}^{n=\infty} \frac{Ln(3)}{n^2}$ $Convergent$ $(Comparison\ Test)$

107

6. Use a Test to determine, if possible, convergence/divergence of the series:

a. $\displaystyle\sum_{n=1}^{n=\infty} \frac{\sqrt{n}}{n^3}$ $Divergent(P-series)$

b. $\displaystyle\sum_{n=2}^{n=\infty} \frac{1}{\ln(n)} > \sum_{n=1}^{n=\infty} \frac{1}{n}$ $Divergent(P-series)$

c. $\displaystyle\sum_{n=1}^{n=\infty} \ln(n^{-1}+1)$ $Divergent$ $Lim_{n\to\infty}\int_1^n \ln(t^{-1}+1)dt = \infty$ $Integral\ test$

d. $\displaystyle\sum_{n=1}^{n=\infty} \tan(\frac{1}{n})$ $Divergent$ $\lim_{n\to\infty}\left|\dfrac{\tan(n^{-1})}{n^{-1}}\right| = \lim_{n\to\infty}\left|\dfrac{(\dfrac{-n^{-2}}{\cos^2(n^{-1})})}{-n^{-2}}\right| = 1$ $Limit\ comparison$

e. $\displaystyle\sum_{n=1}^{n=\infty} 12\cdot\left(\frac{81}{80}\right)^n$ $Divergent(Geometric, r>1)$

f. $\displaystyle\sum_{n=1}^{n=\infty} (-1)^n \ln(\frac{1}{n})$ $Divergent$ $\left(\lim_{x\to\infty}(a_n)\neq 0\right)$

g. $\displaystyle\sum_{n=1}^{n=\infty} (-1)^n \ln(\frac{1}{n}+1)$ $Convergent$ $Alternating\,(a_n\to 0)$

h. $\displaystyle\sum_{n=1}^{n=\infty} (-1)^n \sqrt{\sin(\frac{1}{n})}$ $Convergent$ $Alternating\,(a_n\to 0)$

i. $\displaystyle\sum_{n=1}^{n=\infty} \frac{\cos(n\pi)+e^{i\pi n}}{n} = \sum_{n=1}^{n=\infty} \frac{2\cdot(-1)^n}{n}$ $Convergent$ $Alternating\,(a_n\to 0)$

j. $\displaystyle\sum_{n=1}^{n=\infty} \frac{1}{n+\ln(n)}$ $Divergent$ $\lim_{n\to\infty}\left|\dfrac{\dfrac{1}{n+\ln(n)}}{n^{-1}}\right| = 1$ $Limit\ comparison$

k. $\displaystyle\sum_{n=2}^{n=\infty} \frac{1}{n(\ln(n))^2}$ $Convergent$

$Lim_{n\to\infty}\displaystyle\int_2^n \frac{1}{t(\ln(t))^2}dt = Lim_{n\to\infty}\left[-(\ln(t))^{-1}\right]_2^n = \frac{1}{\ln(2)}$ $Integral\ test$

l. $\displaystyle\sum_{n=1}^{n=\infty} \frac{1}{n+\sin(n)} > \sum_{n=1}^{n=\infty} \frac{1}{n+1}$ $Divergent\ (Comparison\ Test)$

m. $\displaystyle\sum_{n=1}^{n=\infty} \frac{n}{n-2^n}$ $\lim_{n\to\infty}\left|\dfrac{\dfrac{n+1}{n+1-2^{n+1}}}{\dfrac{n}{n-2^n}}\right| = \dfrac{1}{2}$ $Convergent\ (Ratio\ test\ )$

n. $\displaystyle\sum_{n=1}^{n=\infty} \frac{n-\dfrac{1}{n}}{n+\dfrac{1}{n}}$ $Divergent\left(\lim_{x\to\infty}(a_n)\neq 0\right)$

108

1.5. – ABSOLUTE/CONDITIONAL CONVERGENCE – ALTERNATING SERIES

1. The **series** $\sum\limits_{n=1}^{\infty} a_n$ is called absolutely convergent if $\sum\limits_{n=1}^{\infty} |a_n|$ is <u>convergent</u>

2. The **series** $\sum\limits_{n=1}^{\infty} a_n$ is called conditionally convergent if $\sum\limits_{n=1}^{\infty} |a_n|$ is divergent but

   $\sum\limits_{n=1}^{\infty} a_n$ is <u>convergent</u>

3. An alternating series is of the form: $\sum\limits_{n=1}^{\infty} (-1)^n a_n \, , \sum\limits_{n=1}^{\infty} (-1)^{n-1} a_n \, , \sum\limits_{n=1}^{\infty} \cos(n\pi) a_n$

4. An alternating series will converge if $Lim_{n\to\infty}(a_n) = 0$

5. For example the series: $\sum\limits_{n=1}^{\infty} \dfrac{1}{n}$ is <u>divergent.</u> However the series $\sum\limits_{n=1}^{\infty} (-1)^n \dfrac{1}{n}$ is

   alternating, its general term tends to $\underline{0}$ and therefore it is <u>convergent</u>. We can say

   that $\sum\limits_{n=1}^{\infty} (-1)^n \dfrac{1}{n}$ is <u>conditionally</u> convergent.

Determine if conditionally convergent, absolutely convergent or divergent:

6. $\sum\limits_{n=1}^{n=\infty} \dfrac{1}{n^3}$ *Absolutely   Convergent*

7. $\sum\limits_{n=1}^{n=\infty} (-1)^n \dfrac{1}{\sqrt[5]{n}}$

   Conditionally   Convergent

8. $\sum\limits_{n=1}^{n=\infty} \cos(n\pi) = \sum\limits_{n=1}^{n=\infty} (-1)^n$ *Divergent*

9. $\sum\limits_{n=1}^{n=\infty} (-1)^{1000+n} \dfrac{1}{n^{0.999}}$

   Conditionally   Convergent

10. $\sum\limits_{n=1}^{n=\infty} 1 + \dfrac{1}{n\sqrt{n}}$ *Divergent*

11. $\sum\limits_{n=1}^{n=\infty} (-1)^n \dfrac{1}{n^{\frac{32}{31}}}$

   Absolutely   Convergent

12. $\sum\limits_{n=1}^{n=\infty} \dfrac{\sin(n\pi)}{\sqrt[7]{n^2}} = 0$

   Absolutely   Convergent

13. $\sum\limits_{n=1}^{n=\infty} (-5)^n$ *Divergent*

14. $\sum\limits_{n=1}^{n=\infty} \dfrac{(-2)^n}{n}$ *Divergent*

15. $\sum\limits_{n=1}^{n=\infty} \left(\dfrac{1}{2}\right)^n$ *Absolutely   Convergent*

16. $\sum\limits_{n=1}^{n=\infty} (-0.9)^n$ *Absolutely   Convergent*

17. $\sum\limits_{n=1}^{n=\infty} \dfrac{(-1)^n \sin(n)}{n}$

   Conditionally   Convergent

18. $\sum\limits_{n=1}^{n=\infty} 1 + \dfrac{3}{n^2}$ *Divergent*

19. $\sum\limits_{n=1}^{n=\infty} 5 \cdot \left(\dfrac{7}{9}\right)^n$ *Absolutely   Convergent*

20. $\sum\limits_{n=1}^{n=\infty} \cos(n\pi + \dfrac{\pi}{2})\sqrt{2n+1} = 0$

   Absolutely   Convergent

21. $\sum\limits_{n=1}^{n=\infty} (-1)^n \sqrt{n}$ *Divergent*

22. $\sum\limits_{n=1}^{n=\infty} 5 \cdot \left(\ln(n) - \ln(2n)\right)^n$

   Absolutely   Convergent

$$\sum_{n=1}^{n=\infty} \sin\left(\frac{1}{n} - n\pi\right) =$$

23. $$\sum_{n=1}^{n=\infty} \sin\left(\frac{1}{n}\right)\cos(n\pi) - \cos\left(\frac{1}{n}\right)\sin(n\pi) =$$

$$\sum_{n=1}^{n=\infty} \sin\left(\frac{1}{n}\right)(-1)^n$$

Conditionally Convergent

24. $$\sum_{n=1}^{n=\infty} \frac{\sin\left(e^{\frac{1}{n}}\right)}{n^2} \quad \text{Absolutely Convergent}$$

25. $$\sum_{n=2}^{n=\infty} \frac{(-1)^n}{\ln(\ln(n))}$$

Conditionally Convergent

26. $$\sum_{n=1}^{n=\infty} \frac{1200(-2)^n}{n \cdot 2^n} = \sum_{n=1}^{n=\infty} \frac{1200(-1)^n}{n}$$

Conditionally Convergent

27. $$\sum_{n=1}^{n=\infty} e^{-\frac{1}{n}} \quad \text{Divergent}$$

28. $$\sum_{n=1}^{n=\infty} 2^{n\ln(n) - n\ln(2n)} = \sum_{n=1}^{n=\infty} \frac{1}{\left(2^{\ln(2)}\right)^n}$$

Absolutely Convergent

29. $$\sum_{n=1}^{n=\infty} \left(-\frac{11}{10}\right)^{n+12} \quad \text{Divergent}$$

30. $$\sum_{n=1}^{\infty} \frac{2n+2}{3n+1} \quad \text{Divergent}$$

31. $$\sum_{n=1}^{\infty} \frac{\ln(e^n)}{n} \quad \text{Divergent}$$

32. $$\sum_{n=2}^{\infty} \frac{\cos\left(e^{\frac{1}{n}}\right)}{\sqrt[3]{n}} \quad \text{Divergent}$$

33. $$\sum_{n=1}^{n=\infty} (-1)^n 2^{-n} \quad \text{Absolutely Convergent}$$

34. $$\sum_{n=1}^{\infty} (-1)^n \frac{n^2 + n}{3n^3}$$

Conditionally Convergent

35. $$\sum_{n=1}^{\infty} \frac{n\sqrt{n^3}}{2\sqrt{n} \cdot n^2}(-1)^n \quad \text{Absolutely Convergent}$$

36. $$\sum_{n=1}^{\infty} Ln\left(\frac{3n^2 + 2n + 1}{5n^2 + 3n + 4}\right) \quad \text{Divergent}$$

37. $$\sum_{n=1}^{\infty} \frac{\cos(n\pi) + n^2}{-n^4} \quad \text{Absolutely Convergent}$$

38. $$\sum_{n=1}^{\infty} \frac{\cos(n\pi)}{\sqrt{n^3}} = \quad \text{Conditionally Convergent}$$

1.6. – POWER SERIES

1. In occasions it is more comfortable to write a certain function.

2. For example the function $f(x) = e^x$ can be written as a power series as follows.

3. The value of the approximation is perfect at x = $\underline{0}$ and differs from it for values that are away from it.

4. In case we approximate the same function around 1:
   As can be seen, here the approximation is perfect at x = e. The higher the degree of approximation is the better the approximation is.

Given the following series, determine their centre and write down the coefficient:

5. $\sum\limits_{n=1}^{n=\infty} x^n$ Centre: 0 $a_n = 1$

6. $\sum\limits_{n=1}^{n=\infty} \frac{1}{n}(x+2)^n$ Centre: -2 $a_n = \frac{1}{n}$

7. $\sum\limits_{n=1}^{n=\infty} \frac{x^n}{\sqrt{n}}$ Centre: 0 $a_n = \frac{1}{\sqrt{n}}$

8. $\sum\limits_{n=1}^{n=\infty} (n+1)(x-2)^n \frac{1}{\sqrt[3]{n}}$ Centre: 2

   $a_n = (n+1)\frac{1}{\sqrt[3]{n}}$

9. $\sum\limits_{n=1}^{n=\infty} \frac{\sin(n)x^n}{n^3}$ Centre: 0

   $a_n = \frac{\sin(n)}{n^3}$

10. $\sum\limits_{k=1}^{k=\infty} \frac{\ln(k)(2x+6)^k}{k^{0.999}}$ Centre: -3

    $a_n = \frac{\ln(k)2^k}{k^{0.999}}$

11. $\sum\limits_{n=1}^{n=\infty} \frac{3^n(3x)^n}{\sqrt{n}}$ Centre: 0

    $a_n = \frac{3^{2n}}{\sqrt{n}}$

12. $\sum\limits_{n=1}^{n=\infty} \frac{(1-x)^n}{n\ln(n)}$ Centre: 1

    $a_n = \frac{1}{n\ln(n)}$

Given the graph of the approximation, write down the centre of the power series

13. Centre: 0

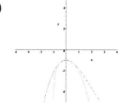

14. Centre: 1.6

15. A power series may not produce a finite value for any value of x, the set of values for which it produces a finite value is called the interval of convergence.

Find the Centre, Interval of Convergence and Radius of Convergence of the following power series:

$$\sum_{n=1}^{n=\infty} e^{-n} x^n \quad Lim_{n\to\infty} \left| \frac{e^{-(n+1)} x^{n+1}}{e^{-n} x^n} \right| = Lim_{n\to\infty} \left| e^{-1} x \right| < 1$$

16. $x = -e \quad \sum_{n=1}^{n=\infty} (-1)^n \quad Divergent \quad x = e \quad \sum_{n=1}^{n=\infty} 1 \quad Divergent$

$Centre : 0 \quad Radius = e \quad Interval \ of \ Convergence : x \in (-e, e)$

$$\sum_{n=1}^{n=\infty} \frac{n(x+4)^n}{2^n} \quad Lim_{n\to\infty} \left| \frac{2^n (n+1)(x+4)^{n+1}}{2^{n+1} n(x+4)^n} \right| = Lim_{n\to\infty} \left| \frac{(x+4)}{2} \right| < 1$$

17. $x = -6 \quad \sum_{n=1}^{n=\infty} \frac{n(-2)^n}{2^n} \quad Divergent \quad x = -2 \quad \sum_{n=1}^{n=\infty} n \quad Divergent$

$Centre : -4 \quad Radius = 2 \quad Interval \ of \ Convergence : x \in (-6, -2)$

$$\sum_{n=1}^{n=\infty} \frac{2^n}{n^2} (x-2)^n \quad Lim_{n\to\infty} \left| \frac{2^{n+1} n^2 (x-2)^{n+1}}{2^n (n+1)^2 (x-2)^n} \right| = Lim_{n\to\infty} \left| 2(x-2) \right| < 1$$

18. $x = \frac{3}{2} \quad \sum_{n=1}^{n=\infty} \frac{2^n}{n^2} (-\frac{1}{2})^n \quad Convergent \quad x = \frac{5}{2} \quad \sum_{n=1}^{n=\infty} \frac{2^n}{n^2} (\frac{1}{2})^n \quad Convergent$

$Centre : 2 \quad Radius = \frac{1}{2} \quad Interval \ of \ Convergence : x \in [\frac{3}{2}, \frac{5}{2}]$

$$\sum_{n=1}^{n=\infty} \frac{3}{4^n n^2} (x+1)^n \quad Lim_{n\to\infty} \left| \frac{3 \cdot 4^n n^2 (x+1)^{n+1}}{4^{n+1} 3(n+1)^2 (x+1)^n} \right| = Lim_{n\to\infty} \left| \frac{x+1}{4} \right| < 1$$

19. $x = -5 \quad \sum_{n=1}^{n=\infty} \frac{3}{4^n n^2} (-4)^n \quad Convergent \quad x = 3 \quad \sum_{n=1}^{n=\infty} \frac{3}{n^2} \quad Convergent$

$Centre : -1 \quad Radius = 4 \quad Interval \ of \ Convergence : x \in [-5, 3]$

$$\sum_{n=1}^{n=\infty} \frac{n^n}{n!} x^n \quad Lim_{n\to\infty} \left| \frac{(n+1)^{n+1} n! x^{n+1}}{n^n (n+1)! x^n} \right| = Lim_{n\to\infty} \left| \frac{(n+1)^n x}{n^n} \right| = Lim_{n\to\infty} |ex| < 1$$

20. $x = -\frac{1}{e} \quad \sum_{n=1}^{n=\infty} \frac{n^n}{n!} (-e)^{-n} \quad Convergent \quad x = \frac{1}{e} \quad \sum_{n=1}^{n=\infty} \frac{n^n}{n!} e^{-n} \quad Convergent$

$Centre : 0 \quad Radius = \frac{1}{e} \quad Interval \ of \ Convergence : x \in [-\frac{1}{e}, \frac{1}{e}]$

21. $\sum_{n=1}^{n=\infty} \frac{n}{3^{n+1} \ln(n)} (x+5)^n$

22. $\sum_{n=1}^{n=\infty} \frac{n}{(Ln(n))^n} (x-2)^n$

23. $\displaystyle\sum_{n=1}^{n=\infty} \frac{2n^2}{5^{n+1}}(2x-2)^n$

24. $\displaystyle\sum_{n=1}^{n=\infty} \frac{n+1}{8^n}(4x-2)^n$

25. $\displaystyle\sum_{n=1}^{n=\infty} \frac{(n+1)}{\ln(n)+5^n}x^n$

1.7. –TAYLOR AND MCLAURIN SERIES

1. In the 18th century The Taylor series (which are power series) used to approximate values of functions were developed.

2. When the value around which (*a*) the series is developed is 0, it is called a <u>Mclaurin</u> series.

3. Find the Taylor Series for sin(x) around the point x = 0. Find 3 – 4 terms, identify the pattern and write it in sigma notation.

$$f(x) = \sin(x) \qquad f(0) = 0$$

$$f'(x) = \cos(x) \qquad f'(0) = 1$$

$$f''(x) = -\sin(x) \qquad f''(0) = 0$$

$$f'''(x) = -\cos(x) \qquad f'''(0) = -1$$

$$f(x) = 0 + \frac{1 \cdot x}{1!} + \frac{0 \cdot x^2}{2!} - \frac{x^3}{3!} + \ldots = \sum_{n=1}^{\infty} \frac{(-1)^{n+1}}{(2n-1)!} x^{2n-1}$$

4. Find the Mclaurin Series for cos(x). Find 3 – 4 terms, identify the pattern and write it in sigma notation.

$$f(x) = \cos(x) \qquad f(0) = 1$$

$$f'(x) = -\sin(x) \qquad f'(0) = 0$$

$$f''(x) = -\cos(x) \qquad f''(0) = -1$$

$$f'''(x) = \sin(x) \qquad f'''(0) = 0$$

$$f(x) = 1 + \frac{0 \cdot x}{1!} - \frac{1 \cdot x^2}{2!} + \frac{0 \cdot x^3}{3!} + \ldots = \sum_{n=1}^{\infty} \frac{(-1)^{n+1}}{(2n-2)!} x^{2n-2} = \sum_{n=0}^{\infty} \frac{(-1)^n}{(2n)!} x^{2n}$$

5. What would be the Taylor Series of $f(x) = 3x^4 + x^3 + 5$ around x = 0?
   A Taylor series is a polynomial therefore the same function will be obtained.
   $$f(x) = 3x^4 + x^3 + 5$$

6. Find the Taylor Series for $f(x) = e^x$ up to 3rd degree around the point x = 1

$$f(x) = e^x \qquad f(1) = e$$

$$f'(x) = e^x \qquad f'(1) = e$$

$$f''(x) = e^x \qquad f''(1) = e \qquad etc.$$

$$f(x) = e + \frac{e \cdot (x-1)}{1!} + \frac{e \cdot (x-1)^2}{2!} + \frac{e \cdot (x-1)^3}{3!} + \ldots = \sum_{n=0}^{\infty} \frac{e}{n!} (x-1)^n$$

7. Find the Taylor Series for $f(x) = \ln(x)$ up to 3rd degree around the point x = 1

$$f(x) = \ln(x) \qquad f(1) = 0$$

$$f'(x) = x^{-1} \qquad f'(1) = 1$$

$$f''(x) = -x^{-2} \qquad f''(1) = -1$$

$$f'''(x) = 2x^{-3} \qquad f'''(1) = 2$$

$$f(x) = 0 + \frac{1 \cdot (x-1)}{1!} - \frac{1 \cdot (x-1)^2}{2!} + \frac{2 \cdot (x-1)^3}{3!} + \ldots$$

8. Find the Taylor Series for $f(x) = \sqrt{x}$ up to 3rd degree around the point x = 2

$$f(x) = x^{\frac{1}{2}} \qquad f(2) = \sqrt{2}$$

$$f'(x) = \frac{1}{2} x^{-\frac{1}{2}} \qquad f'(2) = \frac{1}{2\sqrt{2}}$$

$$f''(x) = -\frac{1}{4} x^{-\frac{3}{2}} \qquad f''(2) = -\frac{1}{8\sqrt{2}}$$

$$f'''(x) = \frac{3}{8} x^{-\frac{5}{2}} \qquad f'''(2) = \frac{3}{32\sqrt{2}}$$

$$f(x) = \sqrt{2} + \frac{(x-2)}{2\sqrt{2}} - \frac{(x-2)^2}{16\sqrt{2}} + \frac{3 \cdot (x-2)^3}{192\sqrt{2}} + ...$$

9. Find the Taylor Series for $f(x) = \dfrac{1}{2-x}$ up to 3rd degree around the point x = −1

$$f(x) = (2-x)^{-1} \qquad f(-1) = \frac{1}{3}$$

$$f'(x) = (2-x)^{-2} \qquad f'(-1) = \frac{1}{9}$$

$$f''(x) = 2(2-x)^{-3} \qquad f''(-1) = \frac{2}{27}$$

$$f'''(x) = 6(2-x)^{-4} \qquad f'''(2) = \frac{6}{81}$$

$$f(x) = \frac{1}{3} + \frac{(x+1)}{9} + \frac{(x+1)^2}{27} + \frac{(x+1)^3}{81} + ...$$

10. Find the Mclaurin Series for $f(x) = x \cdot e^{2x}$ up to 3rd degree.

$$f(x) = xe^{2x} \qquad f(0) = 0$$
$$f'(x) = (1+2x)e^{2x} \qquad f'(0) = 1$$
$$f''(x) = (4+4x)e^{2x} \qquad f''(0) = 4$$
$$f'''(x) = (12+8x)e^{2x} \qquad f''(0) = 12$$
$$f(x) = 0 + x + 2x^2 + 2x^3 + ...$$

11. Find the Mclaurin Series for $f(x) = e^{\sin(x)}$ up to 4th degree.

$$f(x) = e^{\sin(x)} \qquad f(0) = 1$$
$$f'(x) = e^{\sin(x)} \cos(x) \qquad f'(0) = 1$$
$$f''(x) = e^{\sin(x)}(\cos^2(x) - \sin(x)) \qquad f''(0) = 1$$
$$f'''(x) = e^{\sin(x)}(\cos^3(x) - 3\sin(x)\cos(x) - \cos(x)) \qquad f'''(0) = 0$$
$$f^{IV}(x) = e^{\sin(x)}(\cos^4(x) - 6\sin(x)\cos^3(x) + 3\sin^2(x) - 4\cos^2(x) + \sin(x)) \quad f^{IV}(0) = -3$$

$$f(x) = 1 + x + \frac{x^2}{2} - \frac{x^4}{8} + ...$$

12. Find the Mclaurin Series for $f(x) = Ln(\sqrt{x+1}+1)$ up to 2nd degree.

$f(x) = Ln(\sqrt{x+1}+1)$ $\qquad$ $f(0) = Ln(2)$

$f'(x) = \dfrac{1}{2\sqrt{x+1}(\sqrt{x+1}+1)} = \dfrac{1}{2}(x+1+\sqrt{x+1})^{-1}$ $\qquad$ $f'(0) = \dfrac{1}{4}$

$f''(x) = -\dfrac{1}{2}(x+1+\sqrt{x+1})^{-2}(1+\dfrac{1}{2}(x+1)^{-\frac{1}{2}})$ $\qquad$ $f''(0) = -\dfrac{3}{16}$

$f(x) = Ln(2) + \dfrac{1}{4}x - \dfrac{3x^2}{32} + ...$

13. Find the Mclaurin Series for $f(x) = \dfrac{1}{\sin(x+\dfrac{\pi}{2})}$ up to 2nd degree.

$f(x) = \left(\sin(x+\dfrac{\pi}{2})\right)^{-1}$ $\qquad$ $f(0) = 1$

$f'(x) = -\left(\sin(x+\dfrac{\pi}{2})\right)^{-2} \cdot \cos(x+\dfrac{\pi}{2})$ $\qquad$ $f'(0) = 0$

$f''(x) = 2\left(\sin(x+\dfrac{\pi}{2})\right)^{-3} \cdot \cos^2(x+\dfrac{\pi}{2}) + \left(\sin(x+\dfrac{\pi}{2})\right)^{-2}\sin(x+\dfrac{\pi}{2})$ $\quad$ $f''(0) = 1$

$f(x) = 1 + \dfrac{x^2}{2} + ...$

Can be done easier observing that $\sin(x+\dfrac{\pi}{2}) = \cos(x)$

14. Find the Mclaurin Series for $f(x) = (Ln(x+1))^2$ up to 3rd degree.

$f(x) = (Ln(x+1))^2$ $\qquad$ $f(0) = 0$

$f'(x) = \dfrac{2(Ln(x+1))}{x+1}$ $\qquad$ $f'(0) = 0$

$f''(x) = \dfrac{2(x+1)^{-1}(x+1) - 2(Ln(x+1))}{(x+1)^2} = \dfrac{2-2(Ln(x+1))}{(x+1)^2}$ $\quad$ $f''(0) = 2$

$f'''(x) = \dfrac{-2(x+1)^{-1}(x+1)^2 - 2(x+1)(2-2(Ln(x+1)))}{(x+1)^4}$ $\qquad$ $f''(0) = -6$

$f(x) = x^2 - x^3 + ...$

15. Find the Mclaurin Series for $f(x) = e^{\ln(x+1)+1}$, can you explain your answer?

Since the function can be written in the following way:

$f(x) = e^{\ln(x+1)+1} = e^{\ln(x+1)}e^1 = (x+1)e = ex + e$

This is its Mclauring series: $ex + e$

LAGRANGE FORMULA FOR THE ERROR

$$R_n(x) \leq \left| \frac{f^{(n+1)}(c)}{(n+1)!}(x-a)^{n+1} \right|, \text{ c is a number between a and x that maximizes } f^{(n+1)}$$

1. Find the value of sin(1) and maximum error committed on approximating sin(1) using the Taylor series up to 3rd degree around 0 of $f(x) = \sin(x)$

$$f(x) = \sin(x) \quad f(0) = 0 \quad f'(x) = \cos(x) \quad f'(0) = 1 \quad f''(x) = -\sin(x) \quad f''(0) = 0$$

$$f'''(x) = -\cos(x) \quad f'''(0) = -1 \quad f(1) = 0 + \frac{1 \cdot 1}{1!} + \frac{0 \cdot 1^2}{2!} - \frac{1^3}{3!} = \frac{5}{6} \quad f^4(x) = \sin(x)$$

$$R_3(1) \leq \left| \frac{f^{(4)}(c)}{4!}1^4 \right| = \left| \frac{\sin(1)}{4!}1^4 \right| = \frac{\sin(1)}{24} < \frac{1}{24} \quad (f^4(1) = \sin(1) \ (Highest))$$

$$\left| \sin(1) - \frac{5}{6} \right| \approx 0.00814 < \frac{1}{24} \approx 0.0417$$

2. Find the value of ln(2) and the maximum error committed on approximating ln(2) using the Taylor series up to 3rd degree around 0 of $f(x) = \ln(x+1)$.

$$f(x) = \ln(x+1) \quad f(0) = 0 \quad f'(x) = (x+1)^{-1} \quad f'(0) = 1 \quad f''(x) = -(x+1)^{-2}$$

$$f''(0) = -1 \quad f'''(x) = 2(x+1)^{-3} \quad f'''(0) = 2 \quad f(x) = 0 + \frac{1 \cdot x}{1!} - \frac{1 \cdot x^2}{2!} + \frac{2 \cdot x^3}{3!} + ...$$

$$\ln(1+1) = \ln(2) = f(1) = \frac{1 \cdot 1}{1!} - \frac{1 \cdot 1^2}{2!} + \frac{2 \cdot 1^3}{3!} = \frac{5}{6} \quad f^4(x) = -6(x+1)^{-4}$$

$$R_3(1) \leq \left| \frac{f^4(c)}{4!}1^4 \right| = \left| \frac{-6}{4!}1^4 \right| = \frac{1}{4} \quad (f^4(0) = -6 \ (Highest))$$

$$\left| \ln(2) - \frac{5}{6} \right| \approx 0.140 < \frac{1}{4} = 0.25$$

3. Find the value of ln(2) and the maximum error committed on approximating ln(2) using the Taylor series up to 2nd degree around 0 of $f(x) = \ln(1+\sin(x))$. What value should be plugged into x?

$$f(x) = \ln(1+\sin(x)) \quad f(0) = 0 \quad f'(x) = (1+\sin(x))^{-1}\cos(x) \quad f'(0) = 1$$

$$f''(x) = -(1+\sin(x))^{-2}\cos^2(x) - (1+\sin(x))^{-1}\sin(x) \quad f''(0) = -1$$

$$f(x) = 0 + \frac{1 \cdot x}{1!} - \frac{1 \cdot x^2}{2!} \quad \ln(1+1) = \ln(2) = f(\frac{\pi}{2}) = \frac{\pi}{2} - \frac{\pi^2}{8}$$

$$f^3(x) = 2(1+\sin(x))^{-3}\cos^3(x) + 2(1+\sin(x))^{-2}\cos(x)\sin(x) +$$

$$(1+\sin(x))^{-2}\cos(x)\sin(x) - (1+\sin(x))^{-1}\cos(x) \quad f^3(0) = 1$$

$$R_2(\frac{\pi}{2}) \leq \left| \frac{f^3(c)}{3!}\left(\frac{\pi}{2}\right)^3 \right| = \left| \frac{1}{3!}\left(\frac{\pi}{2}\right)^3 \right| = \frac{\pi^3}{48} \quad (f^3(0) = 1 \ (Highest - GDC))$$

$$\left| \ln(2) - (\frac{\pi}{2} - \frac{\pi^2}{8}) \right| \approx 0.356 < \frac{\pi^3}{48} \approx 0.646$$

2.1. – CONTINUITY AND DIFFERENTIABILITY

The function f(x) = |x| has the following aspect:
Since we do not know how to differentiate absolute value we write the

function as a piecewise function: $f(x) = \begin{cases} -x, x < 0 \\ x, x \geq 0 \end{cases}$

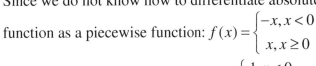

Now we can differentiate it: $f'(x) = \begin{cases} 1, x < 0 \\ -1, x \geq 0 \end{cases}$

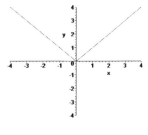

As can be seen the function is continuous at <u>x = 0</u> the derivative however is <u>discontinuous</u> at <u>x = 0</u>. This function is therefore not differentiable at x = 0.

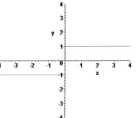

1. Intuitively, a function that is not "smooth" is not differentiable at a point because it's not possible to find a <u>tangent</u> to it at that point.
2. (**T**/F) a discontinuous function will have a discontinuous derivative.
3. (T/**F**) a discontinuous derivative will correspond to a discontinuous function.
4. Differentiability is a property of a function at a <u>point</u> called a local property.
5. For a function to be differentiable at a point first it **must** be <u>continuous</u> at that point.
6. State the condition for <u>continuity of a function</u> at a point where x = a:
    $$Lim_{x \to a^-}(f(x)) = Lim_{x \to a^+}(f(x)) = f(a)$$
7. State the condition for <u>continuity of the derivative</u> at a point where x = a:
    $$Lim_{x \to a^-}(f'(x)) = Lim_{x \to a^+}(f'(x))$$
8. State the **conditions** for <u>differentiability of a function</u> at a point where x = a:
    $$Lim_{x \to a^-}(f(x)) = Lim_{x \to a^+}(f(x)) = f(a)$$
    $$Lim_{x \to a^-}(f'(x)) = Lim_{x \to a^+}(f'(x))$$
9. Fill the table with corresponding graphs of functions:

	f'(x) continuous at c	f'(x) discontinuous at c
f(x) continuous at c	 	
f(x) discontinuous at c	Not possible	

10. Given the function:

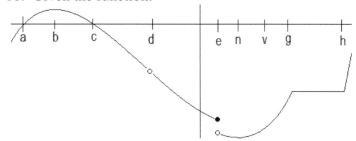

Complete the table:

Fill with:	x	$x = a$	$x = b$	$x = c$	$x = d$	$x = e$	$x = n$	$x = v$	$x = g$	$x = h$
0, + or −	$f(x)$	0	+	-	D.E.	-	-	-	-	-
0, + , −, Doesn't exist	$f'(x)$	+	0	-	D.E	D.E	0	+	D.E	D.E
Cont. or Discon.	$f(x)$	C	C	C	DC	DC	C	C	C	C
Cont. or Discon.	$f'(x)$	C	C	C	DC	DC	C	C	DC	DC
Differ. or Not Differ.	$f(x)$	D	D	D	ND	ND	D	D	ND	ND

11. There are <u>3</u> types of discontinuities:

I. <u>Removable Discontinuity</u>. Sketch an example:
II. <u>Finite jump Discontinuity</u> Sketch an example:
III. <u>Infinite jump Discontinuity</u> Sketch an example:

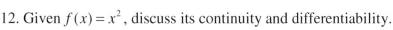
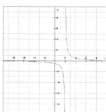

12. Given $f(x) = x^2$, discuss its continuity and differentiability.

f(x) is a polynomial and therefore continuous and differentiable $\forall x \in \mathbb{R}$

13. Given $f(x) = \dfrac{1}{x-2}$, discuss its continuity and differentiability.

$Domain: x \in \mathbb{R}, x \neq 2$

$Lim_{x \to 2^-}(f(x)) = -\infty \qquad Lim_{x \to 2^+}(f(x)) = \infty \qquad f(2) = D.E.$

$f(x)$ is continuous $\forall x \in \mathbb{R}, x \neq 2$, at x = 2 Infinite jump discontinuity

$f(x)$ is differentiable $\forall x \in \mathbb{R}, x \neq 2$

14. Given $f(x) = \dfrac{x-2}{x-2}$, discuss its continuity and differentiability. Sketch it.

$Domain: x \in \mathbb{R}, x \neq 2$

$Lim_{x \to 2^-}(f(x)) = 1 = Lim_{x \to 2^+}(f(x)) = 1 \qquad f(2) = D.E.$

$f(x)$ is continuous $\forall x \in \mathbb{R}, x \neq 2$, at x = 2 Removable discontinuity

$f(x)$ is differentiable $\forall x \in \mathbb{R}, x \neq 2$

15. Given $f(x) = \dfrac{(x-1)(x+2)}{x+2}$, discuss its continuity and differentiability. Sketch it

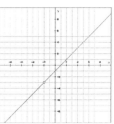

Domain: $x \in \mathbb{R}, x \neq -2$

$Lim_{x \to -2^-}(f(x)) = -3 = Lim_{x \to -2^+}(f(x)) = -3 \qquad f(-2) = D.E.$

$f(x)$ is continuous $\forall x \in \mathbb{R}, x \neq -2$, at $x = 2$ Removable discontinuity

$f(x)$ is differentiable $\forall x \in \mathbb{R}, x \neq -2$

16. Discuss continuity and differentiability of:

$f(x) = \begin{cases} 2 & x < 2 \\ x & 2 \leq x \end{cases}$

Domain: $x \in \mathbb{R}$

$Lim_{x \to 2^-}(f(x)) = 2 = Lim_{x \to 2^+}(f(x)) = 2 = f(2) = 2$

$f(x)$ is continuous $\forall x \in \mathbb{R}$

$f'(x) = \begin{cases} 0 & x < 2 \\ 1 & x > 2 \end{cases}$

$Lim_{x \to 2^-}(f'(x)) = 0 \neq Lim_{x \to 2^+}(f'(x)) = 1$

$f(x)$ is differentiable $\forall x \in \mathbb{R}, x \neq 2$

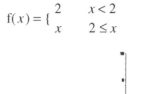

$f(x) = \begin{cases} -x+1 & x < 2 \\ 3 & x = 2 \\ -x+1 & 2 < x \end{cases}$

17. Discuss continuity and differentiability of

Domain: $x \in \mathbb{R}$

$Lim_{x \to 2^-}(f(x)) = -1 = Lim_{x \to 2^+}(f(x)) = -1 \neq f(2) = 3$

$f(x)$ is continuous $\forall x \in \mathbb{R}$, at $x = 2$ Removable discontinuity

$f(x)$ is differentiable $\forall x \in \mathbb{R}, x \neq 2$

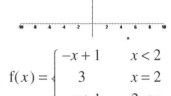

18. Discuss continuity and differentiability of $f(x) = \begin{cases} x^2+1 & x < 1 \\ 2x & 1 \leq x \end{cases}$

Domain: $x \in \mathbb{R}$

$Lim_{x \to 1^-}(f(x)) = 2 = Lim_{x \to 1^+}(f(x)) = 2 = f(1) = 2$

$f(x)$ is continuous $\forall x \in \mathbb{R}$

$f'(x) = \begin{cases} 2x & x < 1 \\ 2 & x > 1 \end{cases}$

$Lim_{x \to 1^-}(f'(x)) = 2 = Lim_{x \to 1^+}(f'(x)) = 2$

$f(x)$ is differentiable $\forall x \in \mathbb{R}$

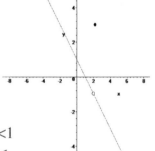

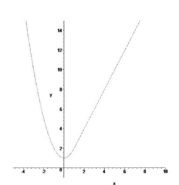

19. Discuss continuity and differentiability of $\quad f(x) = \begin{cases} \ln(x^2) & x < -1 \\ -2x - 2 & -1 \leq x \end{cases}$

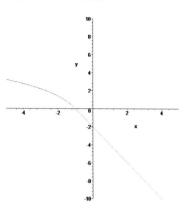

Domain : $x \in \mathbb{R}$

$Lim_{x \to -1^-}(f(x)) = 0 = Lim_{x \to -1^+}(f(x)) = 0 = f(-1) = 0$

$f(x)$ is continuous $\forall x \in \mathbb{R}$

$f'(x) = \begin{cases} 2x^{-1} & x < -1 \\ -2 & x > -1 \end{cases}$

$Lim_{x \to -1^-}(f'(x)) = -2 = Lim_{x \to -1^+}(f'(x)) = -2$

$f(x)$ is differentiable $\forall x \in \mathbb{R}$

20. Given the following function, discuss its continuity and differentiability.

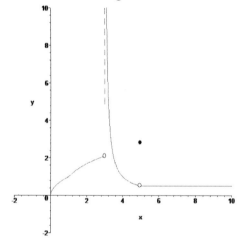

$$f(x) = \begin{cases} \sqrt{x} & x < 1 \\ 1 & x = 1 \\ \ln(x) + 1 & 1 < x \text{ and } x \leq 3 \\ \dfrac{1}{x - 3} & 3 < x \text{ and } x < 5 \\ 3 & x = 5 \\ \dfrac{1}{2} & 5 < x \end{cases}$$

Domain : $x \in \mathbb{R}, x \in [0, 3) \cup (3, \infty)$

$Lim_{x \to 1^-}(f(x)) = 1 = Lim_{x \to 1^+}(f(x)) = 1 = f(1) = 1$

$Lim_{x \to 3^-}(f(x)) = \ln(3) + 1 \neq Lim_{x \to 3^+}(f(x)) = \infty \neq f(3) = 5$

$f(x)$ is continuous $\forall x \in (0, 3) \cup (3, \infty), x \neq 3,$

at x = 3 Infinite jump discontinuity

$f'(x) = \begin{cases} \dfrac{1}{2}x^{-\frac{1}{2}} & x < 1 \\ x^{-1} & 1 < x < 3 \\ -(x-3)^{-2} & 3 < x < 5 \\ 0 & x > 5 \end{cases}$

$Lim_{x \to 1^-}(f'(x)) = \dfrac{1}{2} \neq Lim_{x \to 1^+}(f'(x)) = 1$

$f(x)$ is differentiable $\forall x \in (0, 3) \cup (3, \infty), x \neq 1, 5$

21. Given the following function, find a, and b such that both the function and its derivative will be continuous.

$$f(x) = \begin{cases} a\,x^2 & x < -1 \\ 2\,x^3 + b & -1 \le x \end{cases}$$

Domain : $x \in \mathbb{R}$

$Lim_{x \to -1^-}(f(x)) = a = Lim_{x \to -1^+}(f(x)) = -2 + b = f(-1) = -2 + b$

$f(x)$ is continuous $\forall x \in \mathbb{R}$

$$f'(x) = \begin{cases} 2ax & x < -1 \\ 6x^2 & x > -1 \end{cases}$$

$Lim_{x \to -1^-}(f'(x)) = -2a = Lim_{x \to -1^+}(f'(x)) = 6$

$a = -3, b = -1$

22. Given the function, find a, and b such the function is differentiable for any x.
Domain : $x \in \mathbb{R}$

$Lim_{x \to -2^-}(f(x)) = -8a = Lim_{x \to -2^+}(f(x)) = 16 + b = f(-2) = 16 + b$

$f(x)$ is continuous $\forall x \in \mathbb{R}$

$$f(x) = \begin{cases} a\,x^3 & x < -2 \\ 2\,x^2 - 4\,x + b & -2 \le x \end{cases}$$

$$f'(x) = \begin{cases} 3ax^2 & x < -2 \\ 4x - 4 & x > -2 \end{cases}$$

$Lim_{x \to -2^-}(f'(x)) = 12a = Lim_{x \to -2^+}(f'(x)) = -12$

$a = -1, b = -8$

23. Write an expression of function that will have the 3 different discontinuities at the points where x = –3, 1 and 5. Sketch the function.

$$f'(x) = \begin{cases} 1 & x < -3 \\ 2 & x = -3 \\ 1 & -3 < x \le 1 \\ 2 & 1 < x < 5 \\ \dfrac{1}{x-5} & x \ge 5 \end{cases}$$

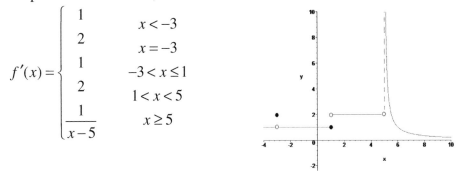

24. Given the following function, find a, b, c and d so that the function is differentiable for any x.

Domain : $x \in \mathbb{R}$

$Lim_{x \to 1^-}(f(x)) = 3 - a = Lim_{x \to 1^+}(f(x)) = b = f(1)$

$Lim_{x \to 4^-}(f(x)) = 16b = Lim_{x \to 4^+}(f(x)) = -16c - 16 + d = f(4)$

$f(x)$ is continuous $\forall x \in \mathbb{R}$

$$f(x) = \begin{cases} 3\,x - a & x < 1 \\ b\,x^2 & 1 \le x \text{ and } x < 4 \\ -c\,x^2 - 4\,x + d & 4 \le x \end{cases}$$

$$f'(x) = \begin{cases} 3 & x < 1 \\ 2bx & 1 < x < 4 \\ -2cx - 4 & x > 4 \end{cases}$$

$Lim_{x \to 1^-}(f'(x)) = 3 = Lim_{x \to 1^+}(f'(x)) = 2b$

$Lim_{x \to 4^-}(f'(x)) = 8b = Lim_{x \to 4^+}(f'(x)) = -8c - 4$

$b = \dfrac{3}{2}, c = -2, a = \dfrac{3}{2}, d = 8$

2.2. – ROLLE AND MEAN VALUE THEOREMS

1. **Rolle's Theorem** if $f(x)$ is a continuous on (a, b), differentiable on $[a, b]$ and $f(a) = f(b)$ the there is at least one point in (a, b) with $f'(c) = 0$

2. Graphically it can be seen in the following graph:

3. In case the function is discontinuous or not differentiable theorem does not hold as can be seen in the following graphs:

4. Given the function $f(x) = \sin(e^x)$.

    a. Given that $f(x) = \dfrac{1}{2}$, find the x values that solve this equation in $(-1,1)$

    $\dfrac{1}{2} = \sin(e^x)$ $\dfrac{\pi}{6} = e^x$ $x_1 = \ln(\dfrac{\pi}{6}) \approx -0.647$ $\dfrac{5\pi}{6} = e^x$ $x_2 = \ln(\dfrac{5\pi}{6}) \approx 0.962$

    b. In consequence show that Rolle's Theorem is satisfied by finding the point where the derivative is 0 in this interval.

    $f'(x) = \cos(e^x)e^x = 0$ $e^x = \dfrac{\pi}{2}$ $x = \ln(\dfrac{\pi}{2}) \approx 0.452$ Rolle T. is satisfied.

5. Given the function $f(x) = x^2 \ln(x^2)$.

    a. Given that $f(x) = e$, find all the x values that solve this equation.
    Using GDC (representing graphs searching for intersections):
    $f(x) = x^2 \ln(x^2) = e$ $x = \pm 1.65$

    b. In consequence show that the Rolle's Theorem is satisfied by finding the point where the derivative is 0.

    $f'(x) = 2x\ln(x^2) + 2x = 0; 2x(\ln(x^2) + 1) = 0; x = \pm e^{-\frac{1}{2}} \approx \pm 0.607$
    The theorem is not really satisfied because f(x) is not defined at 0.

6. Given the function $f(x) = |\ln(x)| = \begin{cases} \ln(x) & x < 0 \\ -\ln(x) & x > 0 \end{cases}$.

    a. Given that $f(x) = 2$, find all the x value that solve this equation.
    $f(x) = |\ln(x)| = 2; x_1 = e^2; x_1 = e^{-2}$

    b. In consequence explain why does Rolle's Theorem is not satisfied in this case.
    The Theorem is not satisfied because at x = 1 f(x) is not differentiable, f(1) = 0 is well defined but the derivative f'(1) does not exist.

7. Given the function $f(x) = 5\sin(\dfrac{5}{x} + \dfrac{1}{2})$.

    a. Given that $f(x) = 4$, find the 2 biggest solutions for x that solve this equation.
    Using GDC (representing graphs searching for intersections)
    $f(x) = 5\sin(\dfrac{5}{x} + \dfrac{1}{2}) = 4$ $x_1 = 11.7$ $x_2 = 2.92$

    b. In consequence show that the Rolle's Theorem is satisfied by finding the point where the derivative is 0 between the 2 points found in part a.

    $f'(x) = -25x^{-2} \cos(\dfrac{5}{x} + \dfrac{1}{2}) = 0$ $x = 4.67$

8. **The Mean Value Theorem:** if $f(x)$ is a continuous on (a, b), differentiable on $[a, b]$ then there is at least one point in (a, b) with $f'(c) = \dfrac{f(b) - f(a)}{b - a}$

9. Graphically it can be seen in the following graph:

10. In case the function is discontinuous or not differentiable theorem does not hold as can be seen in the following graphs:

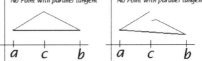

11. Given the function $f(x) = e^x, x \in [0, \ln(2)]$.

   a. Find the average slope between 0 and ln(2). $\dfrac{2-1}{\ln(2)-0} = \dfrac{1}{\ln(2)} \approx 1.44$

   b. Find a point in the same interval in which the tangent will have the same slope to show that the Mean value theorem is true.

   $f'(x) = e^x = \left(\ln(2)\right)^{-1}$ $x = \ln\left(\left(\ln(2)\right)^{-1}\right) \approx 0.367$ The point is $(-\ln(\ln(2)), \left(\ln(2)\right)^{-1})$

12. Given the function $f(x) = \sin(x) + x, x \in [\pi, 2\pi]$.

   a. Find the average slope between π and 2π. $\dfrac{2\pi - \pi}{2\pi - \pi} = 1$

   c. Find a point in the same interval in which the tangent will have this slope to show that the Mean value theorem is true.

   $f'(x) = \cos(x) + 1 = 1$ $x = \dfrac{3\pi}{2}$ The point is $(\dfrac{3\pi}{2}, \dfrac{3\pi}{2} - 1)$

13. Given the function $f(x) = \tan(x), x \in [\pi, 2\pi]$.

   a. Find the average slope between π and 2π. $\dfrac{0-0}{2\pi - \pi} = 0$

   b. Show that there is no point in the same interval in which the tangent will have this slope, explain why the mean value theorem is not satisfied in this case.

   $f'(x) = \left(\cos(x)\right)^{-2}$ *No Solution*, Tan(x) is not continuous not differentiable

   at $x = \dfrac{3\pi}{2}$ and therefore the theorem is not satisfied.

14. Given the function $f(x) = \dfrac{1}{x}, x \in [1, 2]$.

   a. Find the average slope between 1 and 2. $\dfrac{1 - \dfrac{1}{2}}{2 - 1} = -\dfrac{1}{2}$

   b. Find a point in the same interval in which the tangent will have this slope.

   $f'(x) = -x^{-2} = -\dfrac{1}{2}, x = \sqrt{2} \approx 1.41$ The point is $(\sqrt{2}, \dfrac{1}{\sqrt{2}})$

2.3. – RIEMANN SUMS

1. A Riemann sum is a method to find the area "under" a function.

2. Approximate the area of the function $f(x) = x$ between 0 and 5 using 5 intervals of corresponding lengths both using the "upper sum" and "lower sum" approximations.

Lower Sum: $0 + 1 + 2 + 3 + 4 = 10$

Upper Sum: $1 + 2 + 3 + 4 + 5 = 15$

True Value: 12.5

3. Approximate the area of the function $f(x) = \sqrt{x}$ between 1 and 3 using 4 intervals of corresponding lengths both using the "upper sum" and "lower sum" approximations.

Lower Sum: $\frac{1}{2}(1 + \sqrt{1.5} + \sqrt{2} + \sqrt{2.5}) \approx 2.61$

Upper Sum: $\frac{1}{2}(\sqrt{1.5} + \sqrt{2} + \sqrt{2.5} + \sqrt{3}) \approx 2.97$

True Value: ≈ 2.78

4. Approximate the area of the function $f(x) = \frac{1}{x}$ between 1 and 4 using 6 intervals of corresponding lengths both using the "upper sum" and "lower sum" approximations.

Lower Sum: $\frac{1}{2}(\frac{2}{3} + \frac{1}{2} + \frac{2}{5} + \frac{1}{3} + \frac{2}{7} + \frac{1}{4}) = \frac{341}{280} \approx 1.22$

Upper Sum: $\frac{1}{2}(1 + \frac{2}{3} + \frac{1}{2} + \frac{2}{5} + \frac{1}{3} + \frac{2}{7}) = \frac{223}{140} \approx 1.59$

True Value: ≈ 1.38

2.4. – FUNDAMENTAL THEOREM OF CALCULUS

The fundamental theorem of Calculus is usually stated in two parts.

$$F'(x) = \frac{d}{dx}\int_a^x f(t)dt = f(x)$$

Exercises: Find the derivatives of each of the following functions:

1. $F(x) = \int_a^x \sin(t)dt \qquad f(x) = \sin(x) =$

2. $F(x) = \int_a^x t^2 dt \qquad f(x) = x^2$

3. $F(x) = \int_2^x \ln(t)dt \qquad f(x) = \ln(x)$

4. $F(x) = \int_{-3}^x \arctan(\cos(t)\ln(t^2))dt \qquad f(x) = \arctan(\cos(x)\ln(x^2))$

5. $F(x) = \int_3^8 \sin(t)dt \qquad f(x) = 0$

6. $F(x) = \int_x^8 \sin(t)dt = -\int_8^x \sin(t)dt \qquad f(x) = -\sin(x)$

7. $F(x) = \int_x^8 e^{3\cos(t)}dt = -\int_8^x e^{3\cos(t)}dt \qquad f(x) = -e^{3\cos(x)}$

8. $F(x) = \int_0^8 \sin^2(t)dt \qquad f(x) = 0$

Evaluate:

9. $\dfrac{d}{dx}\displaystyle\int_a^x \dfrac{2}{3t^3+4}dt = \dfrac{2}{3x^3+4} =$

10. $\dfrac{d}{dx}\displaystyle\int_0^x \dfrac{2}{3t^2+4}dt = \dfrac{2}{3x^2+4} =$

2.5. – IMPROPER INTEGRALS

1. In occasions we need to evaluate an area that extends to infinity. Find the following improper integrals:

2. $\int_{2}^{\infty} e^{-x} dx = \left[-e^{-x}\right]_{2}^{\infty} = \left[\lim_{x \to \infty} \left(-e^{-x}\right) - \left(-e^{-2}\right)\right] = e^{-2}$

3. $\int_{0}^{\infty} e^{-0.1x} dx = \left[-10e^{-x}\right]_{0}^{\infty} = \left[\lim_{x \to \infty} \left(-10e^{-x}\right) - \left(-10\right)\right] = 10$

4. $\int_{1}^{\infty} \frac{1}{x} dx = \left[\ln(x)\right]_{1}^{\infty} = \left[\lim_{x \to \infty} \left(Ln(x)\right) - \left(0\right)\right] = \infty$

5. $\int_{1}^{\infty} \frac{1}{x^2} dx = \left[-x^{-1}\right]_{1}^{\infty} = \left[\lim_{x \to \infty} \left(-x^{-1}\right) - \left(-1\right)\right] = 1$

6. $\int_{1}^{\infty} \frac{1}{(2x+3)^4} dx = \left[\frac{(2x+3)^{-3}}{-6}\right]_{1}^{\infty} = \left[\lim_{x \to \infty} \left(\frac{(2x+3)^{-3}}{-6}\right) - \left(\frac{1}{-750}\right)\right] = \frac{1}{750}$

7. $\int_{2}^{\infty} \frac{1}{x\sqrt{x}} dx = \left[-2x^{-\frac{1}{2}}\right]_{2}^{\infty} = \left[\lim_{x \to \infty} \left(-2x^{-\frac{1}{2}}\right) - \left(-\frac{2}{\sqrt{2}}\right)\right] = \sqrt{2}$

8. $\int_{0}^{\infty} e^{-x} dx = \left[-e^{-x}\right]_{0}^{\infty} = \left[Lim_{x \to \infty}\left(-e^{-x}\right)\right] - \left[-e^{-0}\right] = 0 + 1 = 1$

9. $\int_{1}^{\infty} Ln(x)dx = \int_{1}^{\infty} xLn(x) - x\, dx = \left[xLn(x) - x\right]_{1}^{\infty} = \left[Lim_{x \to \infty}\left(x(Ln(x) - 1)\right)\right] - \left[-1\right] = \infty$ (by parts)

10. $\int_{3}^{\infty} \frac{\ln(x)}{x^2} dx = \left[-\frac{Ln(x)}{x} - \frac{1}{x}\right]_{3}^{\infty} = \left[Lim_{x \to \infty}\left(-\frac{Ln(x)}{x} - \frac{1}{x}\right)\right] - \left[-\frac{Ln(3)}{3} - \frac{1}{3}\right] = \frac{Ln(3)}{3} + \frac{1}{3}$
(by parts)

11. $\int_{0}^{\infty} \frac{1}{1+x^2} dx = \left[\arctan(x)\right]_{0}^{\infty} = \left[Lim_{x \to \infty}\left(\arctan(x)\right)\right] - \left[0\right] = \frac{\pi}{2}$

12. $\int_{1}^{\infty} \frac{1}{x(1+Ln(x))} dx = \left[Ln(1+Ln(x))\right]_{0}^{\infty} = \left[Lim_{x \to \infty}\left(Ln(1+Ln(x))\right)\right] - \left[0\right] = \infty$

13. $\int_{1}^{\infty} \frac{1}{x^p} dx = \left[\frac{x^{1-p}}{1-p}\right]_{1}^{\infty} = \left[Lim_{x \to \infty}\left(\frac{x^{1-p}}{1-p}\right)\right] - \left[\frac{1}{1-p}\right] = \frac{1}{p-1}$ (if p > 1, if p ≤ 1, divergent)

14. $\int_{0}^{\infty} xe^{-x} dx = \left[-(x+1)e^{-x}\right]_{0}^{\infty} = \left[Lim_{x \to \infty}\left(-(x+1)e^{-x}\right)\right] - \left[-1\right] = 1$ (By parts)

15. $\int_{0}^{\infty} x^2 e^{-x} dx = \left[-(2+2x+x^2)e^{-x}\right]_{0}^{\infty} = \left[Lim_{x \to \infty}\left(-(2+2x+x^2)e^{-x}\right)\right] - \left[-2\right] = 2$

16. $\int_{1}^{\infty} x^n Ln(x)dx = \left[\frac{x^{n+1}Ln(x)}{n+1} - \frac{x^{n+1}}{(n+1)^2}\right]_{1}^{\infty} =$

$\left[Lim_{x \to \infty}\left(\frac{x^{n+1}Ln(x)}{n+1} - \frac{x^{n+1}}{(n+1)^2}\right)\right] - \left[-\frac{1}{(n+1)^2}\right] = \frac{1}{(n+1)^2}$

Result is valid in case $n < -1$, in case $n \geq -1$ divergent.

3.1. – INTRODUCTION TO DIFFERENTIAL EQUATIONS

1. A differential equation is an equation that relates a function with its <u>derivatives</u>.

2. For example, the derivative of $f(x) = e^x + C$ is $f'(x) = \dfrac{df}{dx} = e^x$. The corresponding

    differential equation is $f(x) = \dfrac{df}{dx} = f'(x) = e^x$.

3. Given the function $f(x) = e^{-x}$. Write a corresponding differential equation that will

    relate the function with its derivative. $f(x) = e^{-x} = -\dfrac{df}{dx} = -f'(x) = -(-e^{-x})$

4. Verify that $f(x) = \dfrac{a}{1 + \ln(x)} + C$ is a solution of $f(x) = -x(\ln(x) + 1) f'(x)$

    $$f'(x) = \dfrac{-a}{x(1 + \ln(x))^2}$$

    $$-x(\ln(x) + 1) f'(x) = -x(\ln(x) + 1) \dfrac{-a}{x(1 + \ln(x))^2} = \dfrac{a}{(1 + \ln(x))} = f(x)$$

5. Given the function $f(x) = \sin(x)$. Write a differential corresponding equation that
    will relate the function with its 2nd derivative.

    $$f(x) = \sin(x)$$
    $$f'(x) = \cos(x)$$
    $$f''(x) = -\sin(x)$$

    $$f(x) = -f''(x) \quad or \quad f(x) = -\dfrac{d^2 f}{dx^2}$$

6. Given the function $f(x) = \dfrac{1}{x}$. Write a corresponding differential equation that will

    relate the function with its 1st derivative. Part of the solution is: $f(x) = f'(x) \cdot \underline{\quad}$

    $$f(x) = \dfrac{1}{x} = x^{-1}$$
    $$f'(x) = -x^{-2}$$

    $$f(x) = -xf'(x) \quad or \quad f(x) = -x\dfrac{df}{dx}$$

3.2. – SLOPE FIELDS

1. Given the following differential equation $f'(x) = \dfrac{df}{dx} = x - y$. This means that the value of the slope of the tangent to the curve is the difference of the coordinates of the point. For example at the point (2, 2) the value of the slope is <u>0</u>. At the point (0, 2) the value of the slope is <u>-2</u> etc. This allows us to graph the family of curves that form the solution by sketching a "little slope" at the sufficiently large number of points:

   The solution of the differential equation is any of the curves produced (one is sketched as an example)

   Draw the slope field that corresponds to each one of the differential equations, add one curve and one isocline to your sketch.

2. $\dfrac{dy}{dx} = y$

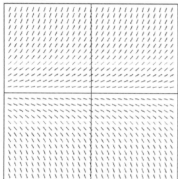

3. $\dfrac{dy}{dx} = x^2$

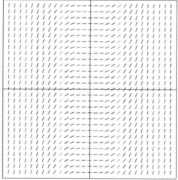

4. $\dfrac{dy}{dx} = y + x$

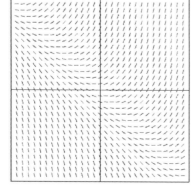

5. $\dfrac{df}{dx} = \dfrac{y}{x}$

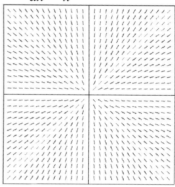

6. $\dfrac{df}{dx} = 2 - y$

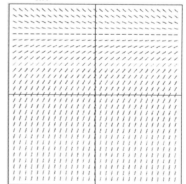

7. $\dfrac{df}{dx} = x^2 + y$

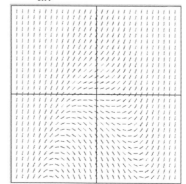

8. $\dfrac{dy}{dx} = 2^x$

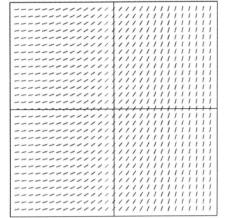

11. $\dfrac{dy}{dx} = \sin(x)$

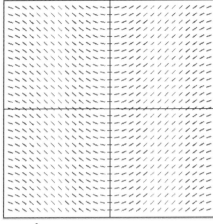

9. $\dfrac{dy}{dx} = x^2 + y^2$

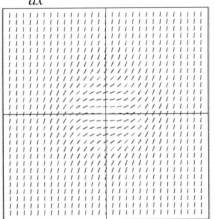

12. $\dfrac{dy}{dx} = \ln(x)$

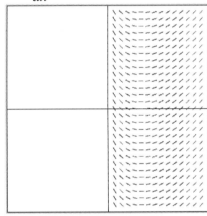

10. $\dfrac{dy}{dx} = \dfrac{1}{y}$

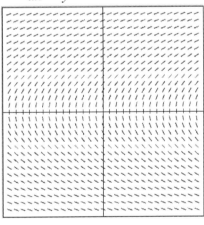

13. $\dfrac{dy}{dx} = \tan(x)$

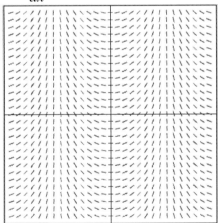

3.3. – EULER'S METHOD

1. Leonard Euler has developed a method to solve differential equations numerically by approximation to the solution.

2. $\dfrac{dy}{dx} = x - e^y$ using Euler's method.

3. $\dfrac{dy}{dx} = x^2 + y$, initial conditions x = 0, y = 1. Use 5 steps to estimate value at x = 0.5.

Step number	0	1	2	3	4	5
x	0	0.1	0.2	0.3	0.4	0.5
y	1	1.1	1.211	1.3361	1.4787	1.6426
$\dfrac{df}{dx}$	1	1.11	1.251	1.4261	1.6387	1.8926

4. $\dfrac{df}{dx} = \ln(x^2) - y^2$ Initial conditions x = −1, y = 0. Use 4 steps, estimate value at x = −0.2.

Step number	0	1	2	3	4
x	−1	−0.8	−0.6	−0.4	−0.2
y	0	0	−0.0893	−0.2952	−0.6791
$\dfrac{df}{dx}$	0	−0.4463	−1.030	−1.920	−3.680

5. $\dfrac{df}{dx} = \dfrac{1}{x} + y$ Initial conditions x = 1, y = 1. Use 5 steps to estimate value at x = 2.

Step number	0	1	2	3	4	5
x	1	1.2	1.4	1.6	1.8	2
y	1	1.4	1.8467	2.3589	2.9556	3.6579
$\dfrac{df}{dx}$	2	2.233	2.561	2.984	3.511	4.158

6. $\dfrac{df}{dx} = \dfrac{y}{x+y}$ Initial conditions x = 0, y = 1. Use 5 steps to estimate value at x = 0.5.

Step number	0	1	2	3	4	5
x	0	0.1	0.2	0.3	0.4	0.5
y	1	1.1	1.1917	1.2773	1.3583	1.4355
$\dfrac{df}{dx}$	1	0.9167	0.8562	0.8098	0.7725	0.7417

3.4. – SEPERABLE DIFFERENTIAL EQUATIONS

1. A separable differential equation is an equation like the one seen the previous part, where the parts in "x" and "y" can be separated and integration take place on both sides of the equation. Solve the differential equations that are separable, if possible express y in terms of x:

2. $\dfrac{dy}{dx} = 1; dy = dx; y = x + C$

3. $\dfrac{dy}{dx} = 2xy; \dfrac{dy}{y} = 2xdx; Ln(y) = x^2 + C; y = e^{(x^2+C)} = ke^{(x^2)}$

4. $\dfrac{dy}{dx} = \dfrac{x+y}{y}$; Cannot be separated. (These equations should be solved using x/y = z, which will be seen in the next chapter).

5. $\dfrac{dy}{dx} = \dfrac{x}{y}$; $ydy = xdx; \dfrac{y^2}{2} = \dfrac{x^2}{2} + C; y = \sqrt{\dfrac{x^2}{2} + C}$

6. $\dfrac{dy}{dx} = x + \ln(y)$; Cannot be separated, beyond extension of course.

7. $\dfrac{1}{x} \cdot \dfrac{dy}{dx} = y \cdot e^x; \dfrac{dy}{y} = x \cdot e^x dx; Ln(y) = (x-1)e^x + C; y = e^{((x-1)e^x+C)} = ke^{((x-1)e^x)}$

8. $(1+x^2)\dfrac{dy}{dx} = y; \dfrac{dy}{y} = \dfrac{dx}{1+x^2}; Ln(y) = \arctan(x) + C; y = e^{\arctan(x)+C} = ke^{\arctan(x)}$

9. $\dfrac{dy}{dx} = xy + \dfrac{x}{y}; \dfrac{dy}{dx} = x(y + \dfrac{1}{y}); \left(\dfrac{y}{y^2+1}\right)dy = xdx; \dfrac{Ln(y^2+1)}{2} = \dfrac{x^2}{2} + C; y = \sqrt{e^{x^2+2C}-1}$

10. $\dfrac{dy}{dx} = \dfrac{e^{2x}+1}{y^2}; y^2dy = (e^{2x}+1)dx; \dfrac{y^3}{3} = \dfrac{e^{2x}}{2} + x + C; y = \sqrt[3]{3\left(\dfrac{e^{2x}}{2} + x + C\right)}$

11. $\dfrac{dy}{dx} = \dfrac{1}{\sin(y)\sqrt{1-x^2}}; \sin(y)dy = \dfrac{dx}{\sqrt{1-x^2}}; -\cos(y) = \arcsin(x) + C; y = \arccos(-\arcsin(x)-C)$

12. $\dfrac{dy}{dx} = \dfrac{xe^{2xy}}{2}$; Cannot be separated, beyond extension of course.

13. $\dfrac{dy}{dx} = e^{2x+y}; \dfrac{dy}{dx} = e^{2x}e^y; e^{-y}dy = e^{2x}dx; -e^{-y} = \dfrac{e^{2x}}{2} + C; y = -Ln(-\dfrac{e^{2x}}{2} + C)$

14. $\dfrac{dy}{dx} = x\tan(y); \tan(y)dy = xdx; -Ln(\cos(y)) = \dfrac{x^2}{2} + C; y = \arccos(e^{\left(-\frac{x^2}{2}-C\right)})$

15. $\dfrac{dy}{dx} = xy^2; \dfrac{dy}{y^2} = xdx; -y^{-1} = \dfrac{x^2}{2} + C; y = \left(-\dfrac{x^2}{2} - C\right)^{-1}$

16. $\dfrac{dy}{dx} = \dfrac{\sec(y)}{y(3x+4)}; \cos(y)ydy = \dfrac{dx}{(3x+4)}; \cos(y) + y\sin(y) + C = \dfrac{Ln(3x+4)}{3};$

    $x = \dfrac{1}{3}\left(e^{3(\cos(y)+y\sin(y)+C)} - 4\right)$ x can be given in terms of y only

17. $\dfrac{dy}{dx} = x + y$ Cannot be separated, can be solved using integrating factor seen later.

3.5. – HOMOGENEOUS DIFFERENTIAL EQUATIONS

1. A homogeneous differential equation is one that can be reduced to a separable by doing the change of variable $v = \dfrac{y}{x}$ $\quad \dfrac{dy}{dx} = v + x\dfrac{dv}{dx}$

2. Solve the following by separating the variables and using the change $v = \dfrac{y}{x}$.

$$\frac{dy}{dx} = \frac{y}{x}; \frac{dy}{y} = \frac{dx}{x}; Ln(y) = Ln(x) + C; y = e^{Ln(x)+C} = kx \text{ (Separation of variables)}$$

$$\frac{dy}{dx} = \frac{y}{x}; v + x\frac{dv}{dx} = v; x\frac{dv}{dx} = 0; dv = 0; v = C; \frac{y}{x} = C; y = Cx \text{ (Change of variable)}$$

Solve the following equations (Separable or homogeneous), if possible express y in terms of x or alternatively x in terms of y.

3.
$$\frac{dy}{dx} = \frac{y^2 + xy}{x^2}; \frac{dy}{dx} = \left(\frac{y}{x}\right)^2 + \left(\frac{y}{x}\right); v + x\frac{dv}{dx} = v^2 + v; x\frac{dv}{dx} = v^2; \frac{dv}{v^2} = \frac{dx}{x};$$
Homogeneous

$$-\frac{1}{v} = Ln(x) + C; -\frac{x}{y} = Ln(x) + C; y = -\frac{x}{Ln(x) + C}$$

4.
$$\frac{dy}{dx} = \frac{y}{x+y}; \frac{dx}{dy} = \frac{x+y}{y}; \frac{dx}{dy} = \frac{x}{y} + 1; \frac{1}{v + x\frac{dv}{dx}} = \frac{1}{v} + 1; 1 = \left(\frac{1}{v} + 1\right)\left(v + x\frac{dv}{dx}\right)$$

$$1 = 1 + \frac{xdv}{vdx} + v + \frac{xdv}{dx}; 0 = \frac{xdv}{dx}\left(\frac{1}{v} + v + 1\right);$$

$$\frac{dx}{x} = dv\left(\frac{1}{v} + v + 1\right); Ln(x) = Ln(v) + \frac{v^2}{2} + v + C;$$

$$Ln(x) = Ln\left(\frac{y}{x}\right) + \frac{y^2}{2x^2} + \frac{y}{x} + C$$
Homogeneous

5.
$$\frac{dy}{dx} = xy + \frac{x}{y}; \frac{dy}{dx} = x\left(y + \frac{1}{y}\right); \frac{ydy}{y^2 + 1} = xdx; Ln(y^2 + 1) = \frac{x^2}{2} + C; y = \sqrt{e^{\left(\frac{x^2}{2} + C\right)} - 1}$$
Separable

6.
$$\frac{dy}{dx} = \frac{y^2 + x^2 + xy}{x^2}; \frac{dy}{dx} = \left(\frac{y}{x}\right)^2 + 1 + \frac{y}{x}; v + x\frac{dv}{dx} = v^2 + v + 1; \frac{dv}{v^2 + 1} = \frac{dx}{x};$$

$$arc\tan(v) = Ln(x) + C; arc\tan\left(\frac{y}{x}\right) = Ln(x) + C; y = x\tan(Ln(x) + C)$$
Homogeneous

7.
$$\frac{dy}{dx} = e^{2x+y}; \frac{dy}{dx} = e^{2x}e^{y}; e^{-y}dy = e^{2x}dx; -e^{-y} = \frac{e^{2x}}{2} + C; y = -Ln\left(-\frac{e^{2x}}{2} + C\right)$$
Separable

8. $$\frac{dy}{dx}=\frac{y^2+x^2-xy}{x^2};\frac{dy}{dx}=\left(\frac{y}{x}\right)^2+1-\frac{y}{x};v+x\frac{dv}{dx}=v^2-v+1;\frac{dv}{v^2-2v+1}=\frac{dx}{x};$$

$$\frac{dv}{(v-1)^2}=\frac{dx}{x};-(v-1)^{-1}=Ln(x)+C;-(\frac{y}{x}-1)^{-1}=Ln(x)+C;y=\frac{x\left(Ln(x)-1+C\right)}{Ln(x)+C}$$

Homogeneous

9. $$\frac{dy}{dx}=\frac{e^{2x}+1}{y^2};y^2dy=\left(e^{2x}+1\right)dx;\frac{y^3}{3}=\frac{e^{2x}}{2}+x+C;y=\sqrt[3]{3\left(\frac{e^{2x}}{2}+x+C\right)}$$

Separable

10. $$\frac{dy}{dx}=\frac{y}{x}+e^{\frac{y}{x}};v+x\frac{dv}{dx}=v+e^v;x\frac{dv}{dx}=e^v;e^{-v}dv=\frac{dx}{x};-e^{-v}=Ln(x)+C$$

$$e^{-\frac{y}{x}}=-Ln(x)-C;y=-xLn(-Ln(x)-C)$$

Homogeneous

11. $$\frac{dy}{dx}=\frac{1}{sin(y)\sqrt{1-x^2}};sin(y)dy=\frac{dx}{\sqrt{1-x^2}};-cos(y)=arcsin(x)+C;y=arccos(-arcsin(x)-C)$$

Separable

12. $$\frac{dy}{dx}=\frac{yxe^{2x}}{2};\frac{2dy}{y}=xe^{2x}dx;2Ln(y)=\frac{1}{4}(2x-1)e^{2x}+C;y=e^{\frac{1}{8}(2x-1)e^{2x}}$$

Separable

13. $$\frac{dy}{dx}=\frac{x^2y+6y^3}{x^3+y^2x};\frac{dy}{dx}=\frac{\frac{y}{x}+6\left(\frac{y}{x}\right)^3}{1+\left(\frac{y}{x}\right)^2};v+x\frac{dv}{dx}=\frac{v+6v^3}{1+v^2};x\frac{dv}{dx}=\frac{v+6v^3-v(1+v^2)}{1+v^2};$$

$$x\frac{dv}{dx}=\frac{5v^3}{1+v^2};\frac{dx}{x}=\frac{1+v^2}{5v^3}dv;\frac{dx}{x}=\frac{1}{5}(v^{-3}+v^{-1})dv;Ln(x)+C=\frac{1}{5}(\frac{v^{-2}}{-2}+Ln(v));$$

$$Ln(x)+C=\frac{1}{5}(\frac{x^2}{-2y^2}+Ln(\frac{y}{x}));$$

Homogeneous

14. $$\frac{dy}{dx}=x\tan(y);\frac{dy}{\tan(y)}=xdx;Ln(sin(y))=\frac{x^2}{2}+C;y=arcsin(e^{\left(\frac{x^2}{2}+C\right)})$$

Separable

15. $$\frac{dy}{dx}=\ln(x)y^2;\frac{dy}{y^2}=\ln(x)dx;\frac{-1}{y}=xLn(x)-x+C;y=\frac{-1}{xLn(x)-x+C}$$

Separable

16. $$\frac{dy}{dx}=\frac{sec(y)}{y(3x+4)};cos(y)ydy=\frac{dx}{(3x+4)};cos(y)+ysin(y)+C=\frac{Ln(3x+4)}{3};$$

$$x=\frac{1}{3}\left(e^{3(cos(y)+ysin(y)+C)}-4\right)\qquad \text{x can be given in terms of y only}$$

Separable

3.6. – INTEGRATING FACTOR

1. Differential equations that have the form: $y' + M(x)y = Q(x)$

2. The idea behind is that we **multiply both sides** of the equation by this factor, $U(x)$,

   the left side of the equation becomes **the derivative of** $y \cdot U(x) : U(x) = e^{\int M(x)dx}$

3. Solve the following differential equations using an integrating factor and then by separation of variables, make sure the same result is obtained.

   By integrating factor:

$$y' + xy = x; U(x) = e^{\int x\,dx} = e^{\frac{x^2}{2}}; e^{\frac{x^2}{2}}y' + e^{\frac{x^2}{2}}xy = xe^{\frac{x^2}{2}}; \left(e^{\frac{x^2}{2}}y\right)' = xe^{\frac{x^2}{2}}$$

$$e^{\frac{x^2}{2}}y = e^{\frac{x^2}{2}} + C; \ y = Ce^{-\frac{x^2}{2}} + 1$$

By separating variables:

$$\frac{dy}{dx} = x(1-y); \frac{dy}{1-y} = x\,dx; -Ln(1-y) = \frac{x^2}{2} + C; \ y = 1 - e^{-\left(\frac{x^2}{2}+C\right)} = 1 - ke^{-\left(\frac{x^2}{2}\right)}$$

Solve the following differential equations using an integrating factor:

4. $y' + y = e^x; U(x) = e^{\int 1\,dx} = e^x; e^x y' + e^x y = e^{2x}; \left(e^x y\right)' = e^{2x}; e^x y = \frac{1}{2}e^{2x} + C; \ y = \frac{1}{2}e^x + Ce^{-x}$

5. $y' = \sin(2x) - y; \ y' + y = \sin(2x); U(x) = e^{\int 1\,dx} = e^x; e^x y' + e^x y = e^x \sin(2x);$

   $\left(e^x y\right)' = \sin(2x); e^x y = e^x\left(\frac{-2}{5}\cos(2x) + \frac{1}{5}\sin(2x)\right) + C;$

   $y = \left(\frac{-2}{5}\cos(2x) + \frac{1}{5}\sin(2x)\right) + Ce^{-x}$

6. $y' + \frac{y}{x} = x^2; U(x) = e^{\int x^{-1}dx} = e^{\ln(x)} = x; xy' + y = x^3; (xy)' = x^3;$

   $xy = \frac{x^4}{4} + C; \ y = \frac{x^3}{4} + \frac{C}{x};$

7. $y' + y = x \cdot e^x; U(x) = e^{\int 1\,dx} = e^x; e^x y' + e^x y = xe^{2x}; (e^x y)' = xe^{2x}$

   $e^x y = \frac{1}{4}e^{2x}(2x-1) + C; \ y = \frac{1}{4}e^x(2x-1) + Ce^{-x}$

8.

$$x\frac{dy}{dx}=\frac{1}{x}-y; \ y'+\frac{1}{x}y=\frac{1}{x^2}; U(x)=e^{\int x^{-1}dx}=e^{Ln(x)}=x; \ xy'+y=\frac{1}{x};(xy)'=\frac{1}{x}$$

$$xy=Ln(x)+C; \ y=\frac{Ln(x)+C}{x}$$

9.

$$xy'+2y=\frac{1}{x^2}; \ y'+\frac{2}{x}y=\frac{1}{x^3}; U(x)=e^{\int 2x^{-1}dx}=e^{2Ln(x)}=x^2; \ x^2y'+2xy=\frac{1}{x};$$

$$(x^2y)'=\frac{1}{x}; \ x^2y=Ln(x)+C; \ y=\frac{Ln(x)+C}{x^2}$$

10.

$$\frac{dy}{dx}=\sin(x)-\frac{y}{x}; \ y'+\frac{y}{x}=\sin(x);U(x)=e^{\int x^{-1}dx}=e^{Ln(x)}=x; \ xy'+y=x\sin(x)$$

$$(xy)'=x\sin(x); \ xy=\sin(x)-x\cos(x)+C; \ y=\frac{\sin(x)-x\cos(x)+C}{x}$$

11.

$$y'+\frac{2y}{x}=e^x;U(x)=e^{\int 2x^{-1}dx}=e^{2Ln(x)}=x^2; \ x^2y'+2xy=x^2e^x;(x^2y)'=x^2e^x$$

$$x^2y=(x^2-2x-2)e^x+C; \ y=\frac{(x^2-2x-2)e^x+C}{x^2}$$

12.

$$\frac{dy}{dx}+\frac{y}{\sqrt{x}}=1;U(x)=e^{\int x^{-\frac{1}{2}}dx}=e^{2\sqrt{x}}; \ e^{2\sqrt{x}}y'+e^{2\sqrt{x}}\frac{y}{\sqrt{x}}=e^{2\sqrt{x}};(e^{2\sqrt{x}}y)'=e^{2\sqrt{x}}$$

$$e^{2\sqrt{x}}y=e^{2\sqrt{x}}(\sqrt{x}-\frac{1}{2})+C; \ y=\sqrt{x}-\frac{1}{2}+\frac{C}{e^{2\sqrt{x}}}$$

13.

$$y'+\frac{2y}{x}=\ln(x);U(x)=e^{\int 2x^{-1}dx}=e^{2Ln(x)}=x^2; \ x^2y'+2xy=x^2Ln(x);$$

$$(x^2y)'=x^2Ln(x); \ x^2y=\frac{1}{3}Ln(x)x^3-\frac{x^3}{9}+C; \ y=\frac{1}{3}Ln(x)x-\frac{x}{9}+\frac{C}{x^2}$$

14.

$$\sqrt{x}y'+2y=x\sqrt{x}; \ y'+\frac{2}{\sqrt{x}}y=x;U(x)=e^{\int 2x^{-\frac{1}{2}}dx}=e^{4\sqrt{x}}; \ e^{4\sqrt{x}}y'+\frac{2e^{4\sqrt{x}}}{\sqrt{x}}y=xe^{4\sqrt{x}};$$

$$(e^{4\sqrt{x}}y)'=xe^{4\sqrt{x}}; \ e^{4\sqrt{x}}y=e^{4\sqrt{x}}(\frac{1}{2}x^{\frac{3}{2}}-\frac{3}{8}x+\frac{3}{16}x^{\frac{1}{2}}-\frac{3}{64})+C;$$

$$y=\frac{1}{2}x^{\frac{3}{2}}-\frac{3}{8}x+\frac{3}{16}x^{\frac{1}{2}}-\frac{3}{64}+Ce^{-4\sqrt{x}}$$